The
Landlord's
Son

Rodney Cam

Disclaimer
This is a true account, although some creative license has been used in
descriptions of people, places and events.

ISBN 978-1-78222-925-4

Book design, layout and production management by Into Print
www.intoprint.net
01604 832149

Contents

The Landlord's Son

Prologue

"He'll never make anything"

These were the words spoken by my father. He was standing behind the Market Room bar of the Brown Cow in conversation with four well-dressed business men standing at the other side. I suppose overheard conversations especially about the evesdropper are never to their advantage. I, meanwhile had my ear pressed to the slightly open roof light on the flat roof which extended across both the Market Room and the central bar. However, actually overhearing this conversation motivated me to improve. It was quite true that up until that point I had achieved very little academically, and at the age of sixteen I had no idea as to what I should do. A levels and a University education was not an option with my mediocre performance so far at school.

The conversation seemed now to be continuing on the lines of what the "old man" (John Robert- Jack to his friends) should do with me. The men whom Jack was probing for information were Directors of Sir Lindsey Parkinson & Co. Ltd a sizeable Engineering company. They had taken a large detached house called Trackwire adjacent to the Brown Cow public house in Whitkirk, an up and coming suburb to the East of Leeds. This house being a convenient location for the men as it was close to Templenewsam the former pile of Lord Halifax, now in the ownership of Leeds City Council who were looking to develop a large marshland area of the estate which bordered the River Aire. In conjunction with the C.E.G.B. (Central Electricity Generating Board) the council were to create ash lagoons in which to deposit the waste product of Skelton Grange power station. The original contract for creating these ash lagoons when completed would elevate the land by some 10 metres was awarded to Cawood Wharton (civil engineering contractors whose head office was located in Harrogate). On commencement of works Cawood Whartons excavations hit a seam of sand and gravel, and in negotiations with the Authorities agreed that the creation of these ash lagoons would be increased in size at no cost to them if the sand and and gravel could be marketed by Cawood Wharton. However, immediately below this layer of sand and gravel they struck coal, the removal of which further increased the capacity of the lagoons. The coal became the responsibility of the National Coal Board who in turn engaged Sir Lindsey Parkinson to carry out all the excavation works and remove the coal. The sand and gravel seam, it was agreed, should be removed and stock piled for Cawood Wharton to screen and market off site. The overburden would be deposited around the excavation sides thus making the lagoons higher and deeper and extending the life of the power station. The only commitment from Cawood Wharton was to create drainage towers to allow the waterborne ash to settle before the water was drained into the river Aire.

The site was a win win situation for everyone and lasted many years, however it never ceases to amaze me that such a project was embarked upon without a Geological Survey.

I know all this because many years later I was employed by Cawood Wharton as a Civil Engineer and one of the sites I was to supervise was the construction of the drainage towers in the ash lagoons.

However, I digress, this overheard conversation changed my attitude to education and how I should conduct the rest of my working life, it was an extreme shock to hear of my fathers opinion of me, not that he had had much to do with either me or my brother's upbringing to that date, nevertheless I held him in high esteem and looked up to him. Shortly after this event I was guided into a profession which I thoroughly enjoyed and achieved moderate success, but it heralded the parting of the ways for the landlord's son.

The Landlord's Son

THE FISHERMAN'S HUT

Chapter 1

Earliest Memories

Some people will tell you that they have memories of the womb or of breast feeding but my earliest memory is of a traumatic incident which occurred at the Fishermans Hut public house in Hunslet, a grimy industrial area close to Leeds city centre. For some reason or other at the age of three I was carrying a jug of ale at the back of the bar, I tripped and fell, the jug broke and a piece of broken porcelain pierced my tongue. "Jack you are supposed to be looking after him" my mother screamed. Blood was streaming from my mouth, I was wrapped in a large towel and bundled into my grandfathers black Austin 12 along with Mum and Dad and my Granddad who was the only one able to drive, not many people could afford a car immediately after World War II but Bertie my grandfather was always interested in motorcars. It was some years later that my Dad eventually took his driving test .

Heated exchanges took place all the way to Leeds Dispensary while I choked on blood and Granddad concentrated on driving. The Leeds Dispensary, a classic terracotta building of the Leeds style on North Street, a small first aid emergency mainly out-patient Hospital, oh how I wish these facilities still existed!

I suppose the most vivid memory is of being rushed into a small tiled entrance and corridor smelling of disinfectant, laid on a rubber covered trolley and wheeled into a room full of intensive light. Those smells of disinfectant and rubber still remain in my memory. What happened next is vague, but I remember my mouth being clamped open and a nurse attempting to put a stitch into my tongue without anaesthetic. I am sure that the event was not as barbaric as that but the trauma is still with me even after the passage of time. Now, in my late seventies I cannot for the life of me understand why the youth of today have their tongues pierced and studs fixed in for cosmetic reasons.

The Fishermans Hut, an unusual name for a public house, presumably so named because of its proximity to the River Aire, although when I lived there I doubt there would be much fish in that polluted waterway with the amount of surrounding industry spewing effluent into it. The site on which the new building was built is remote from the river and I can only assume that where the public house now stands was moved back from the river to allow industrial development to take advantage of the water from the river. The pub did not resemble a hut or a place where fishermen stayed, far from it, it was a red Accrington brick and Portland stone building, its architectural style was that of the twenties and thirties, similar to so many urban public houses built to entertain the working population of these heavily industrialised areas. I assume that the current building was a replacement of an earlier hostelry which would have been by the river. Now located on the corner of Ellerby Lane and East Street in the Hunslet area of Leeds, two storeys and a cellar with plenty of metal framed windows and some with leaded lights, the main feature of the building was a rounded corner of about 12 foot radius made of Portland stone extending to the sill height of the ground floor windows. This rounded corner continued the full height with an ornamental Portland top and a panel displaying the familiar huntsman and the legend "One of Tetley's Houses" this feature hiding a blue slate roof. The Portland stone also featured in a band between the two floors and the window surrounds and mullions, the name of the public house also featured in Portland stone on the semicircular corner. The buildings proximity being just a pavement width separating the building from the two carriageways. To the rear of the building was an Iron foundry and directly opposite on the other side of Ellerby Lane were the remnants of World War 11 air raid shelters with their entrances bricked up but now reopened by the local youth as this area was a great adventure playground on which I also spent time when I was just a little older. Beyond this so called 'oller' was another pub "The Black Dog" this having a glazed tile exterior of black and green bands, goodness knows how this establishment came by its name but I am sure it had nothing to do with Winston Churchill's depressive moods!.

On the opposite side of East Street was a Wesleyan Chapel, now accommodating another form of worship, that of industry as it housed a sheet metal forming company which emitted a cacophony of noise during its hours of operation. Adjacent to this was Ellerby Lane Primary School typical of all school board buildings, stone built, blackened by industrial pollution with high ceilings high windows and two entrances, one with BOYS carved into the lintel above, the other marked GIRLS. For the most part the rest of the immediate district was taken up with rows and rows of brick built back to back terrace houses with cobbled streets which on hot days emitted bubbles of tar from their joints, another source of amusement for the local kids who spent hours bursting them causing their mothers considerable toil in removing it from their skin and clothing.

Chapter 2

B ertie, **my maternal** grandfather was landlord of the 'fish hut', a dapper man about five foot seven tall and always smartly dressed, always wore a waistcoat, with a gold hunter watch in the pocket attached to a gold chain secured through a buttonhole. Clean shaven, hair what was left of it, slicked back, smart suit and polished shoes.

In those days most public houses belonged to the Brewery and this was no exception, but the status of landlord was very important, in a tied house he could hold one of two positions, either that of a Manager or that of a Tenant. A manager worked for the Brewery and received a wage bearing the responsibility for the smooth running of the establishment with all its inherent problems of dealing with the takings, staff, customers, stock and cleaning etc., the tenant on the other hand leased the pub from the Brewery, he was his own boss, owned his own fixtures and fittings, the profit or loss were his, and the only commitment to the Brewery was to sell exclusively their ale. My granddad was the latter.

As a youth he had started his working life at the age of 14 in a leather tannery, but this didn't suit him so he very soon left and got a job in a grocers shop, eventually becoming manager and marrying my Grandmother Florrie, a formidable woman, but more of her later.

At the outbreak of WW1 he joined up as did most able-bodied men in the service of their country and served with the Yorkshire Artillery riding a horse pulling a gun carriage. Like most men who suffered and returned from the first world war he rarely talked about it, but the odd snippets of information we gleaned, he lost part of a finger on his left hand and had two horses shot from under him, saw plenty of action but was one of the lucky ones and returned home after the war, but not before volunteering to stay on to bury his comrades killed in action. My grandmother's sisters, great aunt Susie and great aunt Lizzie, were not so lucky, their husbands great uncle Jim and great uncle Frank never returned. It seemed that during that period no families were untouched by the ravages of this war. The two sisters took a house together in Armley, a suburb of Leeds and spent the rest of their lives together.

Bertie's Commanding Officer was Colonel Eric Tetley (of the brewery family) under whom he served for the duration . On his return, along with his close comrade Bob Barr, they had to make a new start in life. Bob bought a charabanc and begged Bertie to do the same but Bertie had other ideas and asked his old C.O. if any of the brewery properties were available for lease. He was offered and took an off-licence shop in Ramsay Street, Armley, however he did not let his old comrade Bob down and offered to drive

Bobs 'charra' to the coast at weekends. As Bobs business developed he implored Bertie to buy another 'charra' and become partners. Hindsight is a wonderful thing, Bertie refused, preferring to pursue his career in the licence trade, whilst Bob went on to become the founder of the Wallace Arnold Coach company. Oh Bertie, what your grandson could have done with such a start!.

Chapter 3

The interior of the pub had a large central bar formed of polished mahogany panels which served three separate rooms, the floor of the bar was elevated enabling the people serving behind the bar to look down on the customers and in rush times identify who was next to be served. The cellar was accessed through a door at the rear of the bar leading to a flight of steps, this meant that barrels could be changed and general cellar duties carried out without having to walk through the public areas. The counter was also polished mahogany in which the beer pumps were fixed, three banks of three, two bitter one mild serving the three separate rooms. Above the counter was a screen glazed with coloured leaded lights set in a mahogany frame extending to the full height of the ceiling but leaving sufficient gap between counter top and screen to allow easy access to serve customers. This screen in turn concealed a drop-down barrier for use when time was called and the period of service was over. Stringent licensing laws governing opening times were in place and if a landlord did not adhere to these he could lose his licence. Bertie was a stickler for observance of this law and occasionally would lose regular customers to a less law-abiding landlord who would hold 'lock-ins,' a term used to describe when the curtains were drawn, the doors locked and the customers inside would be in for a late-night session. In the days when 'bobbies' walked or cycled round their beat I am sure they were aware that this practice went on but would choose to ignore it in the interests of good public relations, only occasionally making an example of those who ran a disorderly house.

The smallest of the public rooms was the Jug and Bottle, a small passage allowing access to the bar directly from outside. Its purpose was to allow sales of alcoholic beverages to be consumed off the premises, the name Jug & Bottle was derived from a practice no longer pursued, by bringing your own container usually a jug to be filled with draught ale from the pump. Beer sold this way was cheaper than that consumed on the premises and was very popular with the working class who predominantly inhabited the area around the 'Fish Hut'.

Off the lounge was the most intimate of the public rooms 'the snug' still having a terrazzo floor that covered the rest of the public house which afforded easy cleaning. This room had more mahogany wall panelling than the rest of the public house, there was also upholstered seating around the walls and individually upholstered chairs with half a dozen tables again with mahogany tops. Accessed by a half glazed door the room afforded a quieter space for people to drink and engage in intimate conversation.

Chapter 4

On **high days** and holidays my maternal grandmother's large family, she being one of eleven children, three boys, Jess, Ted and Lesley, and eight girls Annie, Fanny, Florrie, Linda, Lizzie, Mary, Sarah and Susie, usually descended on us along with their respective spouses apart from Lizzie and Susie to make a day of it.

The snug was where they usually encamped determined to make the occasion a party. Their children (my half cousins) were dispatched upstairs away from the public rooms to play with 'our Rodney' where we made our own entertainment. I say half cousins because of the age difference in the siblings coming from such a large family meant that these children were really my mother's cousins, but some of them were my age. These occasions were not unwelcome as a great time was had by all and when the regular customers had left and the pub closed my mother would play the piano and a right old sing song ensued.

On one particular Bank Holiday Monday my uncle Ted, well great uncle actually, wandered upstairs to the kitchen to see 'our Joan' (his niece, my mum). "What's that?" Ted asked nodding towards the appetizing smell emanating from the large range just as my mother lifted out a roast joint, and before she could answer Ted had picked up a carving knife and taken off a slice, slipped it between two slices of bread and sidled off back to the family downstairs in the snug. The kitchen was my mums territory as she provided the meals for me and my brother, Grandma, Granddad, and Dad while they ran the pub, although in those days Dad was only part time, his main occupation was an engineering draughtsman at Crofts' a large engineering works in Thornbury, Bradford. Soon the rest of the family seeing Ted's sandwich trooped upstairs with the usual greeting "Hello our Joan that smells lovely" and availed themselves of a sandwich from the joint without so much as a by your leave. Later on in conversation with my dad "just like a set of vultures that lot, but it serves them right, that joint was horse meat for the dogs, greedy beggars!"

My mum's other love apart from the family was her two dogs, a small cairn terrier called Trimmer and a brute of an Alsatian called Bruce. Bruce was a one woman dog, totally obedient and affectionate to one person to the exclusion of all others. He ruled his territory with absolute authority, his job was to guard the premises and he seemed to understand that the general public were allowed in the pub at opening times only. He instinctively knew when opening times were and woe betide anyone found somewhere at a time and place they should not be.

So it was one Sunday when shorter opening times meant that we could go out as a family and the dog was left to roam the premises. What families did on Sunday afternoons in 1947 was visit relatives for afternoon tea. Afternoon teas usually consisted of ham or tongue cut so thin that it became translucent, sandwiched into equal portions of thinly sliced white and brown bread with the crusts cut off. Sometimes, on special occasions, John West tinned salmon and cucumber was used as fillings and cut into delicate triangles. On the occasions we visited my father's brother, uncle Teddy we were treated to first-class baking when my auntie Molly, Teddy's wife, produced the best of all Yorkshire curd tart, or custard tart and scones. Well, she came from a family of commercial bakers.

On our return from our afternoon out the dog could not be found, eventually the he was located on guard at the door of the Gents toilet just off the tap room, dad couldn't move him, and when even my mum was unable to stir him we realised something was amiss. Bertie phoned the police while mum, grandma and me were sent upstairs out of the way. Dad opened the toilet door to find two very contrite frightened would-be thieves only too pleased to surrender themselves rather than be savaged by an eight stone Alsatian desperate to sink his teeth into their legs. The Yorkshire Post carried an article the following Tuesday under the heading: "Burglary attempt foiled by Bruce the brave Alsation", I have often wondered if "brave" was the correct term when two petrified burglars were obviously confined in the right place by a vicious brute of an animal. The apparent intention was that the two men knew that regular Sunday afternoon outings were taken by us as a family being the only free time in the busy life of a publican, and consequently their intention was to hide in the gents toilet at closing time until they knew that the place was unattended and they could carry out the burglary unimpeded and make their escape through the front door. Escape out of the toilet window was not an option as it was heavily barred. Their only alternative was to wait for their apprehension by the local police.

Chapter 5

The keeping of beer is a skill and was more so in the late forties than it is today, even with the resurgence of real ale largely down to CAMRA, (the campaign for real ale). The beer in those days came in wooden casks usually thirty six gallons known as a barrel, but other sizes were available larger being known as a Hogs Head 54 gallons, or smaller known as a Kilderkin 18 gallons or a Firkin 9 gallons or Pin 4.5 gallons.

The Fish Hut cellar could accommodate 12 barrels and the pubs turnover meant that beer was usually delivered weekly by a horse drawn dray, a flat cart pulled by two Shire horses always immaculately turned out. Around this time with increasing motorised traffic Tetley's Brewery benefited from the horse-drawn dray which proved to be an excellent advertisement. However because of the logistics, horse drawn delivery was limited to public houses within three miles of the Brewery. The draymen, two in number, driver and mate, were equally well turned out, brown jackets, shirt and tie and a large leather apron, the sartorial outfit was completed with a brown Billycock, (a bowler hat worn firmly on the head). They rode on a raised sprung bench mounted on the front of the flat cart, this elevated position offering an excellent platform from which to steer the vehicle in and out of the traffic on the narrow streets around the centre of Leeds.

Delivery day was usually on the same day barring Bank Holidays . The dray was drawn up at the side of a trap door set into the ground which gave access to the cellar by a sloping ramp with a narrow flight of steps in between. The barrels were skilfully dropped with a twist of the wrist from the cart onto a padded sack carried for this purpose, and then lowered into the cellar down the ramp restrained by a thick rope placed through an iron ring set into the concrete surrounding the trap door. The barrel end of the rope had two iron hooks which were located into the rim at each end of the barrel, thus allowing the lowering of this heavy object weighing just under 3 hundredweight. Once in the cellar the barrels were rolled into position and again skilfully placed initially onto two parallel steel rails known as the gantry which elevated the horizontal barrel, leaving the bung off the cellar floor and secured with wooden chocks at either side. The draymen continued this operation with all the barrels until the delivery was complete, in the Fish Hut's case usually twelve barrels a week, but on high days and holidays even more. A brass tap was then placed over the bung by either Bertie or my father and driven into the barrel quickly by the use of a wooden mallet so as not to lose any of the contents. A core plug made of hardwood was then driven into the top of the cask to allow the ale to breathe.

Real ale casks them selves carry the brewing sediment and with all this violent activity during its delivery they required at least three days to settle, but on occasions when either Bertie or Jack had miscalculated and the barrels needed to be available for service, then a trick of pumping egg albumen, a solution known in the trade as Fining, into the barrel accelerated the settlement process.

Mother being a softie for all animals except mice always had a treat for the Shires in the form of a mint or a lump of sugar, and Granddad gave the draymen a free pint when their delivery was complete. This in the days of course, when being in charge of a horse and cart with a certain level of alcohol in the blood was not an offence.

The Brewery in those days had a number of tied houses close enough to have delivery by horse drawn dray which in turn meant the brewery maintained a large stable and naturally a turn over of horses. The arrival of a new foal was always an auspicious occasion and with my mothers interest in all animals the ostler asked if the new stallion foal could be named after her first born son, Rodney. Now this is not that in my formative years I resembled a cart horse, in fact quite the reverse, but it was deemed an honour.

After the draymen had left either Bertie or my dad would spend time in the cellar which was a long rectangular room always kept at 60F with a low ceiling and the floor area was half the ground area above. Two steel gantrys at either side, this weeks delivery on one side and the previous weeks on the opposite side. The new delivery had to be left for three days to allow the beer to settle, a bamboo plug was inserted into the hole at the top of the barrel to allow the contents to vent. Just two types of ale was sold, Tetley's bitter and Tetley's dark mild. At the end of the days service the pipes connecting the pump to the barrel would be disconnected and the beer left in them drawn off into a stainless steel bucket. This was not waste but would all be poured back into the dark mild barrel through a large copper filter funnel which rested on four short legs and allowed its delivery pipe to extend into the barrel. This funnel had a filter paper and held about two gallons so was capable of holding the 'draw off' and allowing the beer through the filter to drip back slowly into the mild. Water would then be pulled through the pipes and left clean for the next day. Once a week a caustic soda solution was drawn into all the beer pipes and pumps and left overnight. Both Bertie and my dad took great pride in the quality and clarity of the beer and this contributed in a large part to the success of their tenancy of the Fisherman's Hut.

Chapter 6

My **parents were** married on September 2nd 1940 in the midst of World War 2, Dads occupation that of an Engineering Draughtsman at Croft Engineering in Thornbury, Bradford meant that he was employed on vital work for the war effort, a so-called 'reserved occupation' as Crofts made automotive parts for all types of vehicles necessary to pursue the object of war. My Dad told me many years later that he harboured a feeling of guilt as he was refused his efforts to enlist in the Armed Forces because of his work. His younger brother Teddy on the other hand flew Liberator Bombers, aeroplanes sold to our country from the Americans, and survived the duration of the war even though one of his postings was during the siege of Malta, so Jack supported his brother whenever he could.

Dad worked all the hours he could for Crofts and joined the Volunteer Fire Brigade. Mum and Dads married life began with them living with my grandparents in the pub, so when Jack wasn't at either Crofts or the Fire Brigade he would work in the pub.

Leeds managed to miss most aerial bombardment during World War Two, there were nine raids in all, almost

200 buildings were destroyed, and 64 people lost their lives. Many more buildings were damaged, including some public buildings in the centre of Leeds. There was also a Public House in York Road and fields where a decoy was set up to mislead air attacks on Barnbow, a munitions factory on the Eastern outskirts of the city which still today manufactures Chieftain tanks. In spite of the fact of there being only nine air attacks on Leeds there were many Air-raid warnings, and instead of availing themselves of the purpose-built air-raid shelters on the other side of Ellerby Lane, Bertie, Florrie and Joan would take refuge in the pub cellar whilst Jack did his stint with the volunteer Fire Brigade. On one occasion Jack returned before the all-clear sounded and found the family, including the dogs, down the cellar. "Bloody hell, you lot could be on a cruise". There, sat in striped deck chairs, Bertie and Florrie reading and Joan knitting. "You wouldn't know there was a war on"!

Two years to the month after they were married I put in an appearance, although I have spent my life telling people I was born in a pub, this is not strictly true, I was born in a nursing home in Roundhay Road on the other side of Leeds, but after a short stay was brought home by my doting parents.

Now because local pubs in working class areas in industrial cities were the hub of the community (especially during wartime) it was where service personnel on leave caught up on local gossip. My mum told me as a child that I received more than my share of attention from the locals, so when names were thought of, influence came from all quarters including the regulars, and whether it was a coincidence or not I was named after the battleship Rodney, which in turn received its name from a former Admiral Sir George Brydges Rodney. One of the regulars in the pub was the Boson on the Rodney, and on one occasion when he was on leave he gave me the boson's whistle as a christening present. I have often wondered whether that gift influenced my mother and father's decision on my name. Sadly on one of my parents subsequent house moves it was misplaced and was never seen again. I know the Rodney acquitted itself very well during the war, and was a major part of the operation to sink the Bismarck, one of Germany's major battleships . She survived the duration of the war, but unfortunately I have no knowledge of that boson.

The fourth public room was the Tap room. This was exclusively an all male environment similar in décor to the other rooms but possibly more austere with un-upholstered benches, wooden stools and copper topped Britannia cast iron tables, terrazzo on the floor but still served by the central bar. Access to the Tap room was from a dedicated external door. It was an area where working class men could frequent in their working clothes, and from the adjacent foundry at lunchtime men would replenish the fluid lost in the sweat of working with the furnace, or on an evening after a hard day, to relax with a pint and perhaps a game of dominoes or darts. Domino tables could be fitted over the copper topped tables, these had a peg scoring board at the side for a particular game called 'fives and threes'. In one corner of the room a dart board was fixed with chalk boards at each side and a brass strip let into the floor at the regulation distance from the board. Often inter-pub competitions of darts and dominoes were arranged and the league table produced with trophies eagerly competed for.

I suppose the worst practice in Tap rooms, now thankfully now no longer engaged in, was the use of 'spitoons,' a large brass bucket shaped object with sawdust in the bottom for men to spit into, and it was the job of the poor cleaner to empty these disgusting objects.

I was four years old in January 1947 when the worst winter in living memory hit. This caused traffic chaos, but to a little lad it was fantastic. After the initial snowfall, said to be four foot deep, crisp and white, sadly industrial Leeds soon turned the surface to a murky grey, nevertheless Dad took me sledging to East End Park to a monstrous hill that was all of ten foot high.

It seemed that movement of goods and services came to a halt for at least three days When it was possible for traffic to move again after snow ploughs had cut a channel in some main roads, I recall my mother taking me on a bus into Leeds town centre, however I can only rely on contemporaneous information. Commerce for a substantial period was severely hampered, when even lighter falls of snow cause traffic to grind to a halt today, it seems that nothing changes.

Chapter 7

As soon as I reached the age of five I was able to attend the local junior school, fortunately for me the school was just on the opposite side of East Street. I have little recollection of my time at this junior school but I can remember the layout. There was a central assembly hall with classrooms off to the side, all had very high ceilings and lots of natural light. The assembly hall after morning assembly, was used for physical exercise. It is amazing that the most embarrassing events are the ones printed on ones memory, therefore after one such exercising period, bearing in mind that this was a class of five year olds, the teacher asked if anyone could tie shoe laces as one little girl could not tie her own, and for some reason I said I could "In that case would you oblige" said the teacher, but after some time of struggling with her laces it became apparent that I had exaggerated my ability, and all this in an attempt to impress the girls at the tender age of five.

Less than a year later my brother Michael arrived on the scene. He was also born in the nursing home and it was not long after that mother and baby were brought home to the Fishermans Hut. Being so young I cannot recall my reactions to another human being taking pride of place in the affections of my parents and because of the age discrepancy I didn't really have much to do with my brother, that situation continued until my early 20s. I had my own circle of friends and he had his.

Dad never seemed to spend much time with me or my brother who had made an appearance when I was five and three-quarters. I suppose doing the best for his family during the 1940's meant working all the hours God sent, nevertheless I recall Sunday afternoons when we all walked to East End Park which was about a mile away from the Fisherman's Hut, Dad pushing Michael in the Silver Cross pram (my mothers concession to luxury) which had served me well before I could walk. All this while trying to control me and the two dogs which served to give my mother a rest from domestic chores. Parks in the industrial city are a Victorian legacy for which we should all as a nation be grateful, and East End park was no exception with a well tended area giving way to tennis courts, football pitches and a young children's play area with swings, slides and roundabouts always my favourite. From this park were two roads forbidden to motorised traffic, Black Road and Red Road taking their name from the colour of the material they were surfaced in, one being red shale and the other of black blast furnace ash. Both of these roads were a legacy of the mining and Civil Engineering works that were carried out as mentioned in the prologue. Now being prohibited to traffic they provided a good walk to Templenewsam Park which was a stately home originally founded by the Knights Templars and bequeathed to the City of Leeds by Lord Halifax (the Irwin family). Ironically enough the walk was of such a distance that with two young children and two dogs Dad rarely achieved the full length. Templenewsam is to feature very strongly in my future, but at this time seemed another world away sitting as it did in beautiful green rolling countryside, a stark contrast from the back to back terrace houses around the Fisherman's Hut.

As Dads work increased at Croft Engineering and the pubs business improved we, that is my brother and I, saw less and less of him and eventually all the pressures of work took its toll, with the intricate drawing involved in engineering draughtsmanship Dad lost his eyesight. A period of rest was prescribed and all work had to stop, fortunately his sight returned after three weeks but he never returned to the work he loved at Crofts and wore spectacles for the rest of his life. As a consequence of this and because of the increasing success of the Fisherman's Hut it was agreed that Jack would be an invaluable partner in the life of the pub, so Mum and Dads fate was sealed and was inextricably linked with Florrie and Bertie for the rest of my grandparents lives.

Holidays just after the war were never at the top of peoples agendas and certainly holidays abroad were taken only by the very wealthy or a few hardy adventurous souls, however now there were two families involved in the running of the pub, a seven day a week fifty two weeks a year venture, time off for taking holidays was easily arranged when either Florrie and Bert or Joan and Jack took sole responsibility. Mum and Dad usually managed at least a week away from the pub once a year, always in Blackpool and always at Mrs. Garnetts, a boarding house in York Street just off the Golden Mile. Blackpool's attractions have changed very little over the years and the Golden Mile is no exception, there were the ice cream stalls, the rock shops, amusement arcades with penny slot machines and stalls selling a variety of rubbish the like of 'Souvenir of Blackpool' miniature towers made of pottery whose secondary use was a salt dispenser. There were 'Kiss me Quick' hats and all manner of toys from guns to dolls none of which would last the week. To complete the Golden Mile there was a surfeit of pubs and some say that it was impossible to have a pint in every one without falling over before the end of 'The Mile'. One of the major features of these pubs of an evening were rows of children sitting outside with a bottle of pop and a packet of crisps, incidently the ones with a little blue twist of waxed paper containing salt from which you could season the crisps to your taste, while their parents drank in the licensed premises. Other attractions were the Tower constructed by two Lancashire architects, James Maxwell and Charles Tuke who designed the tower and oversaw the laying of its foundation stone on 29 September 1891. The tower was built at a time when industrial cities were bursting at the seams with workers in factories and mills. As a result a new demand was created for leisure and tourism. Over three thousand people visited the tower on its opening day on 14 May, 1894. From its uppermost platform views for miles of the flat Fylde coast and on a clear day the Isle of Man. Blackpool also had three Piers, South, Central and North all with different amusements to offer, but only the north pier supporting a theatre which in the height of the season attracted the country's top acts.

Another major attraction was the pleasure beach, a must for a visit by our family and in particular the Big Wheel as Croft Engineering produced the gear box designed by my dad which transferred automotive power to make the thing turn. Dad was particularly proud of this and always had to enquire of the operator how it was performing. The pleasure beach, I suppose one of the theme parks which in recent years have sprung up all over the country but at the time I remember it, was quite unique and amongst its many attractions had two enormous roller coasters. We as kids were not allowed to go on the roller coasters but things like the ghost train and the house of fun with its moving floors, distorting mirrors a revolving barrel that challenged even the quickest, but I suppose with the prevalence of health and safety in today's society this would probably not be allowed to operate, but I am convinced that in those days people who chose to enjoy it did so fully in the knowledge that there would be a slight risk and it didn't seem to deter anyone.

The rows of Accrington brick terraced streets were mainly given over to boarding houses and my recollection of a stay in our regular one was one of rules and regulations . I am sure Mrs Garnetts was no exception, the dining room managed to cram enough tables to accommodate all the guests staying at the boarding house at one sitting, the logistics of which would have defied Dr. Who's Tardis. Dinner, if you were posh, or tea if you weren't was taken at six o'clock and consisted of three courses with little or no choice but varied from day to day. The tables were dressed with tablecloth and supported knife, fork, spoon and napkin with ring which along with the table linen had to last the whole week. Permanent features were tomato ketchup, brown sauce and salt and pepper, while Mrs Garnett produced the meals from a tiny back kitchen, Mr. Garnett skilfully manoeuvred his way round the tables serving the food. Rules and regulations in such establishments were paramount as mealtimes should be strictly adhered to, noise at all times should be kept to a minimum, rooms should be vacated by 10am and were not returned to before 5pm. The use of the bathroom and toilet facilities were strictly by rotation as there were not sufficient of these for each family to have their own. Everyone should return from their evening out by 10.30pm and the doors of the boarding house would be locked at 11pm. This practice was laughingly called a 'public service' but I can't imagine hotels and B&B establishments being run on similar lines today.

There were miles of sandy beach which on the odd sunny days filled up with people, dads wearing either flat caps or knotted handkerchiefs, their shirt sleeves rolled up, braces visible and trouser legs rolled up to reveal the whitest legs ever seen, and mums in pretty flowery print dresses with no shoes or nylon stockings relaxing in a striped deck chair which was hired for the whole day. Either one or other parent was seen taking the kids for a paddle ankle deep in the Irish Sea which never seemed to get any deeper no matter how far you walked out into it. My brother and I would spend most of the day in swimming trunks made not from the lightweight materials of today, but of heavy cotton and on occasion wool, and it was not until years later that my wife reminded me that most were hand knitted by parents or grandparents, which once wet, lost all semblance of shape refusing to cover up that which it was supposed to. My memories of times on the beach with Mum, Dad my brother and I would be of Dad carrying two deck chairs, Mum pushing my brothers pushchair with great difficulty through the sand to a spot where a cricket pitch could be marked out for a later game, but eventually the parents settling down, Dad reading daily paper and Mum reading Woman's Own magazine while Michael and I made sand castles, or more to the point I made sand castles and he destroyed them . On odd occasions Dad would join in and construct a magnificent edifice with towers, a moat and a drawbridge, and at other times he would make the shape of a motorcar or a boat in which we could sit.

As young boys, Blackpool offered my brother and I a week of pleasure, sand castles, beach bathing when the weather was fine, the Tower Zoo or amusement arcades if wet or a model aeroplane to make back at the 'digs' but only after 5pm and if we didn't make a mess. On odd evenings a trip on a tram to the Pleasure Beach or one of the many theatres to see a show and we were always allowed to stay up late. Some years we were joined by other families, usually Mum and Dad's friends, and one particular year I remember Uncle Arthur and Aunty Fanny, my mother's family, spending a week with us. Fanny, a stout, short rotund woman and Arthur even shorter, slim and dapper taking particular care of his dress. Fanny and Arthur ran a fish and chip shop in the East End Park region of Leeds and Arthur was always great fun, not having had children of his own, he always had a lot of time for us inventing games and pastimes, whereas Fanny was company for my Mum. Deck chairs were hired by the day and we were usually on the beach by 9 o'clock staking our claim to a section of sand big enough for the odd cricket game or football match, with Arthur and my Dad having divested themselves of jacket and waistcoat, but trousers still with braces attached, legs rolled up, and shoes and socks removed, but in a nod to proprieties of the day Arthur would leave his trilby hat on.

The whole day, weather permitting, would be spent on the beach and lunchtimes would be from a hamper prepared earlier with sandwiches and a flask of warm tea, inevitably the sandwich filling would attract a good amount of sand, there being nowhere to wash hands before lunch. We would wend our way back to the boarding house after an exhausting day of football, cricket, sandcastle building (on other occasions motor cars) donkey rides, ice cream, paddling and one of my favourite occupations, digging a hole big enough to bury my younger brother up to his neck, usually out of sight of parents, but when caught attracted a clip round the ear.

The Fishermans Hut continued to prosper building up a reputation for a well run public house and the senior management of Tetleys Brewery seem to think that Bertie and my father would do well to take on a larger establishment. Eventually, after discussions between my grandfather my father and Tetley senior management, it was agreed that they would take on the tenancy of the Brown Cow at Whitkirk one of the largest public houses in Tetley's ownership, however, the tenancy would not take place immediately, but after two years operating the premises as managers. While this was not the perfect deal, It seemed that the move would be worthwhile and have the potential to be a bigger business than that which the Fishermen Hut offered.

THE BROWN COW

The Landlord's Son

Chapter 1

J**ust before my** 6th birthday I was aware that major changes were about to take place, now at the tender age of 78, I realise why I was not party to any of the discussions but changes that would affect my immediate family were on the cards. A large public house (in fact the jewel in the Tetley Brewery crown) was about to become available. The pub was so large that it would require both my Grandma and Grandpa and Mum and Dad to run it, and although Bertie was a Tenant at the Fish Hut the Brewery would only offer this new undertaking as a managership for an initial period. A further obstacle was that my Mum and Dad would have to commit to living and working with my maternal grandparents for the foreseeable future. On the positive side the Brown Cow, was located in Whitkirk, an up and coming suburb of Leeds, with plenty of middle class houses to the South and West, farmland to the East and Templenewsam the country estate of Lord Halifax to the North. Other points in favour of the move was that the accommodation offered was extensive, so that family members if they so wished could avoid each other for a while, also the move would be away from the industrial heartland of the city and would offer a more pleasant environment for myself and my brother to grow up in.

After much deliberation my parents and grandparents agreed that in spite of having to work for a wage for an initial two year period, the potential to make an exceptional living for all the family was on the cards.

In 1947 when the move was planned, England suffered a tremendous snowstorm with power and transportation being interrupted, I vividly recall the depth of snow in some parts being 3 foot. After a couple of days when local authorities snowploughs had cleared a way and bus services resumed my mother and I went to Leeds town centre where a concerted effort had been made to allow commerce to continue consequently the move was delayed until later we were sure that the delay would be beneficial to all concerned.

So in June 1949 the move from the Fish Hut to the Brown Cow was made.

To a 7 year old the move to Whitkirk seemed like moving to another country, the residential area was a million miles away from the grubby industrial area of Leeds 10.

Chapter 2

The **Brown Cow** a large rustic brick two storey building, mock Georgian in style, with multi-paned arched windows on the ground floor and similar Georgian styled windows on the first floor but having flat lintels. The roof was of green slate and the building was set back at the junction of two major roads, Selby Road and Hollyshaw Lane, the whole site of approximately two acres thus allowing a large car park all the way round with a large garden (eventually to become a beer garden) to the west. The public house, which originally stood on this site was also called the Brown Cow and was an ancient coaching inn and a staging post for a horse-drawn omnibus. It boasted stabling for 40 horses. The public house was purchased by Joshua Tetley and Son in June 1929. The original building was demolished and a new building built set back from the junction. The new development took in the needs that would be required from a public house in a suburb of Leeds, which was expected to grow out of all proportion from the original village.

The first landlord registered at the new property in 1932, was a Mawson Movley and was succeeded by my grandfather in 1949. The living accommodation was spacious forming an L shape, half of the first floor of the building, and a corridor ran along one side lit by natural light from windows opening on to a flat roof area. Off the corridor were a number of rooms. A small single bedroom, mine, a large double bedroom, my grandparents room and a very large sitting room located on the corner, lit by windows from the south and east. A small office occupied mostly during the day by Florrie who kept the books, did most of the paper work and made up the wages. A single bedroom was next, occupied by my brother and then another large double bedroom occupied by my Mum and Dad. At the end of the corridor were two bathrooms and two separate toilets all of which were tiled with white glazed tiles and a green band half way up. These had a very institutional appearance with no hint of luxury but considering that the building was built just after the second world war when most peoples toilet facilities were located outside in a back yard, it was deemed to be the height of sophistication. The other half of the L shaped first floor consisted of a large function room referred to by my family as the "Buff Room" because the Royal Ancient Order of Buffaloes, a mans club on the lines of the Masons and Rotary, met in this room once a week. It was also used for the occasional wedding reception when the catering was done by my mother, and was an ideal location for this type of use as Whitkirk church was immediately opposite. The Buff room when not in public use was used by my mother and I as she played the piano while I sang, and on the occasions of the visits of my Grandmothers enormous family my mother and I would provide the entertainment. "Come on our Joan, give us a tune and our Rodney can sing". My recollection of the most popular song in the repertoire was most inappropriate for a young boy being "In My Sweet Little Alice Blue Gown", but all this was good practice for my membership of the choir at Whitkirk Church. Bringing the upstairs accommodation description to a conclusion was a large kitchen with an enormous Yorkist range with four ovens and eight hobs, gas fired, on which my mother prepared the meals and other food for various functions. This room was lit by windows on two sides to the West and North and had a central table capable of seating 10 people but unlike kitchens of today did not have fitted units but separate preparation tables on the side walls. There were a couple of easy chairs as this room which also provided refuge for my parents and grandparents for the small amount of free time that they had between opening hours, in fact I can hardly recall the use made of the sitting room at the other end of the building apart from the fact that I was incarcerated in there for my piano practice as that room also boasted an upright piano. The kitchen could also be accessed by a door which opened out onto a steel fire escape mainly used by my brother and I and the dogs, two Alsatians by now, as this meant access to the living accommodation without venturing through the public rooms. To one side of the kitchen was a small scullery with a large Belfast sink, no such luxury as dishwashers in those days, this was also lit by a window on each of two sides to the North and East overlooking the flat roof. To complete the layout of upstairs rooms there was a small room which served as a cloakroom when the Buff room was used for public functions, and an even smaller room with no windows which was the wine and spirit store, and this in a pub that could gantry sixty hogsheads (54 gallons) of beer this is indicative proof that pubs in those days sold mainly beer, wines and spirits were drunk only occasionally.

To the South East of the Brown Cow was a general store selling newspapers, cigarettes, and sweets. East of the public house on the other side of Hollyshaw Lane and a unusually shaped roundabout was the Cooperative stores which took the form of a mini department establishment with a furniture department at one end and a grocers and greengrocers sandwiched between the butchers department at the other end. To conclude my description of the accommodation, on the ground floor to the West was a palatial staircase with two flights and a half landing turning through 180 degrees culminating on the ground floor in the main hall. Either side of the half landing were public Ladies and Gents toilets again tiled in those utility white and green banded tiles, however like all public toilets in public houses they had to be kept in good order and it was an obsession with my father to have them immaculate and the cleaners were instructed to maintain them in a spotless condition with even the copper and brass water pipes polished so highly that you could see your distorted reflection in them. The public areas consisted of a large central bar area first approached by a large entrance hall with revolving doors at the front and double swing doors at the rear. On entering by the revolving doors a small smoke room was to your immediate left, moving further in on a 45 degree angled corner inlaid in a mahogany panel was a large Art Deco clock, next comes the wide staircase with access to Ladies and Gents toilets on either side emulating those on the half landing, and then a gents only room . The car park at the rear of the building was accessed by the rear swing doors. Long before the prevalence of mobile telephones the Pub had a payphone located in a small mahogany kiosk which was located at the side of the rear door opposite to the gents only room. Turning back into the hall there was an entrance door into the Market room, this room had special significance to the public house as it had a special licence to serve farmers on market day. The pub probably derives its name from the location as it is immediately in front of the cattle market.

A lounge of similar size to the market room was located on the opposite side of the bar at the front elevation of the pub. It was furnished with basket tables and chairs deemed to be luxurious at the time but a source of annoyance to

Bertie as he was constantly 'shelling out' for ladies snagged nylons. The floor was vinyl and unlike the rest of the pub's floor which was terrazzo, nowhere in the public rooms had a carpet, practicality was the key word rather than luxury, but this didn't deter the clientele as I mentioned before. Whitkirk was becoming a fashionable suburb of Leeds and with little home entertainment, the public house along with the church formed the focal point of the community and as long as the landlord and his immediate family were there to entertain and to serve, then the Brown Cow was the place to go, and the lounge was the place to take your wife to see and be seen at weekends.

The only other public room that I have not yet paid any attention to is the tap room, this room had a separate entrance from the East. Most pubs as I have mentioned before had a taproom, its name originating from when beer was served in hostelries straight from the barrel through a tap, but now was a place for a working man to spend an hour after his working day and did not necessitate a change of clothes. Darts and dominoes were the main pastimes and most regulars would form a team to enter into public house competitions. Without television the way of life was much more interactive and communities benefited from social contact with each other and the pub was the hub. In my opinion it is a shame that we have lost this and lives today don't seem to be as rich because of the electronic age. From the end of the tap room bar was a counter accessed only by the out sales door, this I referred to previously in the description of the Fisherman's Hut as the jug and bottle, but with more and more shops being granted licences to serve alcohol to be consumed off the premises the out sales function of a public house was in decline.

Chapter 3

For a seven year old the move was full of excitement and anticipation, a change of school, my own bedroom, farmland and the Templenewsam estate on the doorstep. The school, Colton County Primary was a total change from what I had been used to. Instead of just across the road it was over a mile away necessitating a bus ride there and back. Sammy Ledgard, the independent bus company's buses were blue, double deckers and old. The most memorable feature was the central pole fixed to the back step to aid alighting and exiting, it was wrapped in white plastic, a source of pending mischief for schoolboys of all ages for unravelling when the conductor wasn't looking. I felt very grown up as I was able to travel to school on my own and pay my own bus fare. It seems that in those days parents bestowed much more trust on their children than they do today but we face no more or less danger and didn't come to any more harm, in fact I believe a certain amount of responsibility at an early age makes a much more rounded individual and somehow leads to teenagers having respect for elders which has been slightly lost in today's society.

Colton County Primary school was a mixture of hard

red brick and stone opened as a Board School in 1876 to offer country children of tenant farmers and land workers an early education, the children of the gentry, squires, lords of the manor, and farmers who owned their own estate sent their children away to boarding school along with children of the professions (clergy, doctors lawyers etc) thus perpetuating the class distinction which was still a major part of the English way of life.

The school had high ceilings with large windows to flood the rooms with natural light. It had a central assembly hall with classrooms off, rooms being divided by half glazed wooden walls. Each classroom was furnished with a large teachers desk at one end of the room, a blackboard behind, and neat rows of wooden desks with sloping hinged lids fixed to iron frames. This practical arrangement of classrooms meant that children sitting at their desks were unable to see into the next classroom but a teacher standing in front of the class was able to do so and thus discipline was maintained even if a teacher in the adjacent class had to leave the room.

Charlie Jackson, an only child, the son of a woodsman working on the Templenewsam estate which was owned at that time by Lord Halifax, lived in the village of Colton in a tied cottage on Chapel Lane. Colton consisted of four tenanted farms and a collection of cottages, some detached some semi-detached and some small terraces along with four or five large detached houses, a chapel, a wooden community hall and the school. Most of these buildings were tenanted as the whole village formed part of the estate. Charlie had been attending Colton County Primary school since he was five and when I arrived at the school he and I struck up a friendship which has continued to this day. We spent most of our leisure time together at either his house or the pub. He lived in the tied cottage with his Mum Muriel (referred to as Mu by his Dad) and his father Fred Jackson. The cottage was semi-detached, solid red brick with a slate roof, very basic single-glazed and heated only by an open fire in the sitting (best) room and a Yorkist range in the kitchen -come -living room on which Mu did all the cooking and it also provided the hot water. The toilet was outside in the yard and all washing of pots and people took place in the scullery off the rear of the living room. Bathing, once a week, was by means of a tin bath brought in from an outhouse and placed in front of the Yorkist range which provided the necessary hot water. In spite of this relative hardship (although not considered so at the time) the cottage always had a comfortable welcoming feel created by Fred and Mu, it afforded extensive views over woods and fields, had a large garden with fruit trees and a vegetable plot which provided the family with all the vegetables and fruit needed on a seasonal basis. I loved spending time at Charlie's house away from the busy roads of Whitkirk riding our bikes or making bogeys. A bogey was a wooden cart with pram wheels and a primitive form of rope steering The front pram wheels and axle were nailed to a piece of 4 x 2 timber with the nails bent over to secure it, the wood then had a hole bored in it by means of a red-hot poker which in turn was attached to the main wooden chassis again with another hole and was attached by means of a large bolt. As time went on and more and more versions of the bogey were built they became more sophisticated with sprung suspension and wheel steering. Early models had no breaking system so shoes were always worn down at the heels, but after many near scrapes and falling off, a breaking system was devised using a pivoted piece of wood applied to the rear wheels with all the force you could muster on steep hills.

The duties of Charlie's Dad Fred as woodsman took him all over the Templenewsam estate, his working attire being brown trousers with the waistband just below his nipple line held up by a pair of braces over a collarless shirt, and just to be sure, a thick leather belt with a brass buckle around his waist which came off occasionally to admonish punishment whenever Charlie stepped out of line, waistcoat and pocket watch on a chain guard with a tweed jacket and a stout pair of working boots completed the outfit. His mode of transport to and from work was a heavy black Raleigh bicycle with his most precious piece of equipment, a billhook, wrapped in sacking and tied with baler twine to the bicycle cross bar. The billhook was a foot-long blade with a reverse hook at the end, the hickory handle to which the blade was attached was about three foot long and the blade and hook were kept razor sharp. To watch Fred lay a hawthorn hedge was to see a master craftsman at work, with a single blow taking out just sufficient wood from the upright growth to allow it to be bent horizontally and staked in place with a sapling Fred had cut from another part of the hedge, all this action taking place at almost walking pace to finish up with a stock-proof hedge. Skills like these have almost died out because of improved mechanised means, but I am not sure they produce as good a finish as Fred did.

In the school holidays Charlie and I would occasionally take Fred his lunch, cycling into the estate woodlands with a cylindrical metal can with a cup-shaped lid and handle, filled with hot tea and a packet of sandwiches wrapped in whatever paper was to hand, usually old newspaper and definitely not the abundant packaging used today. Cycling for young boys was much easier as there was less traffic and these small country roads had not yet achieved rat-run status. The estate was a fantastic playground and during the long summer holidays Charlie and I spent all our time there.

Chapter 4

Bruce the Alsatian was now getting older and was about to find the domain of his new abode changed by a new young pup. The family or should I say mainly my mother, decided that the Brown Cow was too big to be protected by just one dog so the new addition arrived shortly after we took up residence. He (yes another Alsatian dog) came from a litter of nine born on a farm at Castley, a village between Poole and Harrogate, and had the typical sable black and white markings of a German Shepherd and had very large paws, a usually accepted indication that the dog would be large and powerful. I cannot remember how the decision to allow me to be in charge of the new dog was made but in the ensuing years we became the best of pals, and when I was not at school went everywhere together. We named him Flash and as he grew into an adult dog he lived up to his name being extremely agile and able to scale six foot high walls.

At first Bruce didn't take to the new pup but eventually tolerance turned to acceptance, each dog realising that at night time they had separate areas to patrol. Flash's domain was the public rooms and Bruce looked after the family's living accommodation upstairs.

Only once during our twelve years of occupation was there an attempt to burgle the pub. It was a midsummer's night when an intruder broke into the public bar area, these are the years before burglar alarms triggered by movement sensors were freely available. The burglar must have been very quiet as he had managed to get to the central bar area before Flash had heard him. Each evening the tills, of which there were four, had their drawers removed and the takings all in cash were locked away in the upstairs office after their contents had been counted and prepared for banking. Notes of 10 shillings, 1 pound and 5 pounds were bound together in 100 pound bundles held together with gummed paper strips colour-coded for their denomination. Similarly coins, copper, halfpenny, penny and three pence pieces to the value of 1 pound were put in blue paper bags. Silver, sixpence, shilling, two shilling pieces (known as Florins) and half crowns to the value of 5 pounds were put into white paper bags. It was one of these blue paper bags (the only thing resembling cash left behind the bar) which the thief had got his hands on prior to being disturbed He quickly noticed that this bag did not contain cash as my grandfather used this particular coin bag to keep tacks in which he would use for displaying notices around the public house. Realising his predicament when he noticed Flash, the burglar scattered the contents of this bag on the floor hoping to deter the dog while he made his getaway leaping over the taproom bar through the door which he had previously used to gain entry, and ran off down Selby Road. Unfortunately for him he had not counted on Flash's determination to give chase, who ran through the scattered tacks and even with his paws lacerated followed and eventually caught the thief some 100 yards down the road, overpowering him and bringing him to the ground. With all this commotion the sleeping household was roused, the police were summoned and Dad in dressing gown and slippers gave chase and eventually found the terrified burglar with the dog on top of him, teeth bared and paws bleeding.

"Gerrim off me"

"Not a chance until the police arrive" my father said, which they did shortly afterwards and apprehended the felon.

So for the second time one of our guard dogs made the Yorkshire Post. Flash with his story of dedication to duty and in spite of injury to his paws became the hero of the day.

Freedom afforded to 7 year olds in the late 1940's was much more relaxed than it is today, consequently Charlie and I spent most of our free time in the great outdoors, mostly in the woods and fields always accompanied by Flash. We would dam streams, make dens, climb trees and make rope swings and it was not always just the dog Charlie and me, others joined the gang, sometimes there were enough of us to form two separate armies to fight battles, but there were never any girls, as at that age they were of no interest. When the vast acreage of the Templenewsam estate did not have the usual attraction, there was a large garden at the Brown Cow, half of which was given up to a beer garden with wooden tables and benches, the lower half was a vegetable plot with a greenhouse. A large two car garage was built at one end of the high level, accessed from the car park which surrounded the pub and this garden facility was also available as an area for play.

Whitkirk, although steadily being taken over by the now rapidly expanding urban conorbation of Leeds still maintained its village feel . True most of the buildings had been redeveloped over time and were beginning to take on a Fifties modern appearance, but the area still maintained its independent community atmosphere. One thing however was lacking. A Scout hut to accommodate the newly-formed Cub/Scout troop. Bertie recognising this, persuaded Tetleys Brewery to donate a section of the pub garden with a main road frontage to build a Scout hut. In the year of 1950 over a period of six months volunteers cleared the site and erected a corrugated iron Nissan hut with a red brick gable at each end. The front one extended beyond the semi-circular shape of the hut to form a square façade.

It was only a matter of time after the commencement of work on the construction of the Scout Headquarters that Charlie and I found ourselves irresistibly drawn to helping with the build, and from our involvement gained knowledge of what scouting was all about and consequently became Cub Scouts. Just how much use we were at that age is debatable but we had a great time being members of the Cub pack for the next three years.

The Scouts in Whitkirk were run by a husband and wife team Mr and Mrs Willis, he was Skip for the Scouts and she was Akela for the Cubs. A couple dedicated to the Scouting movement, not having children of their own they spent all their spare time encouraging young people in the highest ideals of citizenship. Mrs Willis also ran a Guide troop, but the Scouts and Guides never met and at an age that Charlie and I joined that was not a problem.

Whilst wearing a school uniform was my first taste of conforming to a particular group's rules which has the indicative effect that there is collective responsibility, somehow a Cub uniform meant much more with a strong element of smartness, polished shoes, clean shorts and jumper, clean and neatly ironed neckerchief meticulously worn, held in place with a woggle, and a cap placed correctly on the head. At the start of the meeting the pack was brought to attention arranged in groups of six with a 'sixer' the Cub equivalent of a corporal at its head. Each group of six having their own designated place, so you were not only to keep up a standard for the pack but also for your six. The leaders and helpers of the pack all by tradition took their names from characters out of Kipling's

'Jungle Book' i.e. Akela, Baloo, Shere Khan, Kaa, Mowgli etc.

Chris, a leader, between 18-20 years of age took the name of Baloo the bear, a most unlikely pseudonym for a young man who did not posess any of the characteristics of a bear.

Chapter 5

My first taste of being away from parents was cub camp, a weekend in the Dales which consisted of packing the trailer with all the camping equipment, tents, cooking gear, sleeping bags, ground sheets etc. and setting off one Saturday morning with the trailer hooked up to one of four cars with all the excited cubs distributed among them. This was my first taste of an area of Yorkshire to which I went back again and again, the Dales in my opinion being the most beautiful part of the world and an area which in later life my wife and I chose to spend our retirement. A Scout camp site in Malham was our destination, arriving around lunchtimewhen we all learnt very quickly how to set up camp with just the bare essentials. Nothing sophisticated about the equipment in those days, large canvas bell tents to sleep 8 adults or 10 boys, and needless to say each of the four tents had 8 boys and 1 adult to maintain order and to make sure that the cubs first night away from home did somehow contain some hours of sleep. In spite of the cold rainy weather, burnt sausages cooked on an open fire, and dampers (flour salt and water making a dough, shaped into twists around a stick and placed in the hot embers) when cooked had the burnt outsides broken away and eaten along with the sausages. Sitting on a ground sheet with legs crossed and a plate balanced on our knees we thought this was a meal fit for a King.

We trekked along paths around Malham Cove and Gordale Scar marvelling at the unusual landscape, the leaders pointing out plants, birds and features of the area in general. I loved the whole experience.

Back at HQ the badge system for activities undertaken or skills learnt served to make cub-scouting an addictive experience, all designed to teach potential vandals good citizenship and collective responsibility. The joy of taking home a new well-earned badge for your Mum to sew on your jumper is something all young boys should have the benefit of.

Bob-a-job week came round once a year when the whole movement endeavoured to raise funds for the basic running of each troop. Two, three or more lads for one week of the year offered to carry out tasks for anyone prepared to pay for their labours, usually one shilling (5 new pence). Jobs such as car cleaning, yard sweeping, gardening, and even more unusually Charlie and I had to refill shelves with bottles at the back of the Brown Cow bar ready for the next opening time.

I don't think I have mentioned yet that the time to which I now refer, licensed premises were only allowed to open between 11am and 3pm, and 5pm and 10pm, and any licensee breaking these rules risked losing his licence and consequently his livelihood.

Chapter 6

Charlie's dad, as a young boy, had been a chorister at Whitkirk church, and Charlie's uncle Edgar Skinn was the verger and lived in a tied cottage within the church grounds, so it was natural that Charlie should also become a chorister and consequently, so did I, and from the age of eight and until my voice broke at age 11 I had a fantastic time. I enjoyed singing from an early age and as I have already mentioned was encouraged by my mother who was a decent pianist and a good accompanist. My grounding as a chorister benefited from previous concerts when my maternal grandmother's family encouraged our Joan to play the piano and our Rodney to sing. Before the advent of television people made their own entertainment and family gatherings usually meant those with any modest talent would be encouraged to perform.

Again, because of the lack of technology choirs were very popular, and the choir of Whitkirk church was no exception and had a strong membership. With practice once a week, usually on Wednesday evening and two services on Sunday there were always at least 16 boys and a similar number of men. Boys were paid one and sixpence a week increasing to two shillings for ribbon boys(a medal from the Royal School of Church Music worn on either a blue or red ribbon over the surplus). This elevated status bestowed on the ribbon boy allowed him to lead the procession at the beginning and end of the service, and a responsibility for disciplining the younger choristers. The older boys in the choir usually got the lead parts (descants or solos) as they had more experience which in turn brought more appreciation from the congregation and with it, tips from the older members of the church.

Weddings occasionally would request that the choir be in attendance and sing at the service, and there was never any shortage of volunteers as a fee between 2/6 and 5/- was paid to the choir boys and even more if a solo was sung. I never did find out what the going rate for the men was but I am sure it was much more. I remember with a great deal of pride and satisfaction when I had been a chorister for a number of years, at the end of a well sung service and my turn to sing the solo, a little old lady would come up to me and press a half crown into my grateful palm. Church choir practice was held in St. Mary's room which was a single storey stone built building set in the extensive Vicarage garden. It had a slate roof with a chimney stack at one end, there were windows down either side and entry was gained through an oak door with typical church ironmongery. Once entered there were rows of chairs down either side, an open fireplace opposite the door and an upright piano to the right of the fireplace. It was large enough to hold 30 choristers. Mr. Gilliard, the very accomplished organist and choir master was always first to arrive on practice nights and would have laid out the sheet music on each chair which we were to sing at the forthcoming services that week. Practice for the boys was one hours duration between 6 and 7 and similarly between 7 and 8 for the men. Now, however innocent and angelic choir boys like our group were, we were always up to no good, in activities from playing noughts and crosses or catapulting paper pellets across the choir stalls during the vicars sermon, this on occasions could result in a crack from a male chorister in the choirstall behind or if Gilliard saw from his organ loft mirror at the back of the church, would result in pocket money being docked. It was many years later that I actually saw that mirror put to good use as I walked down the aisle with my new bride on my arm to the strains of Mendelssohn's wedding march, I looked up and saw Gilliard's smiling face framed therein followed by a big thumbs up.

There were however mischievous activities as boys will be boys. Winter meant that a fire would be lit in St. Mary's room and occasionally after the boys practice one of us would climb onto the roof and block the chimney with a grass sods, smoking out the men and resulting in a chase through the Vicarage gardens and out towards Templenewsam with much cursing from the pursuing men. Other notable misdemeanours came about as a result of there being no campanologists to ring the half peal of bells at Whitkirk, so with the usual resourcefulness of young boys, just before each service some of us dressed only in cassocks would climb the spiral staircase of the tower to the ringing chamber and toll the largest bell. In order to exit the ringing chamber in time for the commencement of the service, we had to run down the spiral tower steps out into the churchyard and back into the side door of the vestry, put on our white surplus and ruffle and process into church and take our place in the choir stalls, all before the bell stopped ringing . Eggy (Kenny) Glover the eldest, largest and strongest boy would hold the bell on its stop, then let go the bell rope which would snake about while we ran out.

At the top of the square church tower was a stone castellated parapet, this was built on corbels which left a gap between the lead covered walkway which was a base for the small lead spire surmounted by a weather vane, the gap allowed rain water to drain off, and occasionally two or three boys would climb the rest of the spiral staircase from the ringing chamber to emerge at the top of the tower, and from there would pee on the assembling congregation through the aforementioned gap. The choir boys found it a great laugh to see the unsuspecting putting up umbrellas assuming a short shower of rain. You must understand dear reader that I was never party to this practice and would never own up if I was.

St. Marys church Whitkirk received, and to my knowledge still does receive it' s living from a legacy left by the Knights Templars, a religious order of soldiers founded in 1118 and who eventually owned the land now known as Templenewsam, and as a consequence a service was held once a year as a condition of the legacy, in the chapel at the end of the Great Hall in the magnificent stately home that Templenewsam has now become. The chapel highly decorated with heraldic symbols was lit by stained glass windows containing Biblical scenes, and a small hand-pumped organ which left only enough room to accommodate the Vicar, his attendants and the choir. This annual event always attracted a good congregation who had to be seated on chairs set out in rows in the Great Hall leaving a clear aisle down the centre along which the choir, the Vicar and his attendants in full vestments would process to the chapel and the service would commence. My recollection of these events was of a great occasion on a Sunday in July when the sun always shone.

Another enjoyable bonus of being a choirboy was that once a year there was a choir trip, usually to the coast by coach on a Saturday in Summer. An event which encouraged the boisterous activities that a group of choirboys could get up to. The occasional dip in the sea or a water fight between rowing boats on Peasholm Park Lake with regular breaks for copious quantities of fish and chips and ice cream, which usually ended up with one or two boys being sick on the way home. Now boys will be boys, and it seems that a right of passage to adulthood or even senior adolescence had to be the partaking of alcohol which was somehow smuggled onto the bus before we set off on our journey home. It seemed that tolerance on behalf of the choirmaster and one or two of the other choirmen who accompanied us was the order of the day, and nothing was ever said, leaving us to nurse a sore head the next day.

At Christmas time the choir would go out Carol singing, and apart from singing around Whitkirk would go on to the villages of Colton and Austhorpe, and finally finish in the Brown Cow, where the choir would stand in rows on the large staircase. A piano would be brought into the hall and choirmaster Gilliard would play and the choir would sing the carols. This practice usually collected a fair amount of money which was given to various charities.

The Scouting movement, always keen to demonstrate its affiliation with the Christian organisations, similar to the Armed Forces, would hold regular parades when the Scout troop, Cub pack, Guide troop and Brownie pack would process from the Scout HQ (scout hut) to St. Marys Church in full uniform, a Standard being carried in front of each column. So when you are a member of both organisations, choir and Scouts, a difficult choice had to be made, which usually left the choir depleted on such occasions. To take part in the parade was eagerly anticipated by members of the Scouts, Cub, Guide and Brownie packs and it meant an immaculate turnout with cleaned and pressed uniform, shoes highly polished and being well scrubbed and with well groomed hair, and the parade usually attracted spectators who lined the route along Selby Road with the inevitable attendance of proud Mums and Dads. The event meant that traffic would be halted along Selby Road while the parade passed, a practice I am sure would be impossible today with the abundance of bureauocracy to which we all have to pay lip service. On one occasion I persuaded Skip (the leader of the Scouts and Cubs) to allow Charlie to carry the Cub Standard, the pole of which surmounted by a brass wolf would be secured in a leather holder attached to the wearer by a leather waist band and neck halter. Such was Charlie's eagerness to allow all to see the Standard, he had raised it to such a level that he struck the base of each truss along the South aisle, needless to say he was only ever allowed to be Standard bearer once.

Chapter 7

For the first two years at the Brown Cow Bertie was a manager, this meant that he ran the pub on behalf of the brewery who owned the premises lock stock and barrel, and received a wage just like the rest of the staff which obviously included Mum and Dad. Any improvement in business and consequently profit was to the brewerys advantage, managed houses were quite common at the time as it enabled aspiring licencees to take on a public house without having to come up with the cash for the valuation of stock, fixtures and fittings. In the case of the Brown Cow this was a considerable amount compounded by the fact that a substantial rent was required as the pub was deemed to be the jewel in Tetley's crown.

The majority of public houses in the 50's and 60's were owned by one or other of the breweries, this meant that these pubs known as 'tied houses' would only be allowed to sell the products of that brewery, however in the eighties the Government brought in legislation under the Monopolies Commission that breweries had to dispose of most of the public houses they owned and were sold off to property companies. Now with hindsight this has been a major mistake, as the property companies that purchased this real estate by their nature were bound to produce a good return on their investment which inevitably led to an escalation in the rents. Breweries on the other hand had more of an interest in selling their products and would rather keep the rents at a reasonable level to maintain an outlet for their beer. This change in the way that the brewing industry had been traditionally run has led to a major decline in the number of pubs with one or two closing every week and those able to stay in business had to develop a food orientated business being a major part of their income rather than somewhere that people just went for a drink.

After Bertie's initial two year stint as a manager he was able to convince the brewery that he was capable of running the Brown Cow and more importantly he was able to raise the cash for fixtures, fittings and stock and the advanced period of rent. Once the agreed date had been fixed, two independent valuers specialising in public house valuations would be appointed, one working on behalf of my grandfather and the other for the brewery. So early on the morning of the appointed day the stock would be taken and all the fixtures and fittings would be listed, this included the tables and chairs, the beer pumps, all the glassware, the light fittings, curtains and everything to allow the landlord to run the business. When everything was listed and because on this particular occasion the items were numerous, the pub would open and continue to trade as usual while the two valuers agreed on a figure that my family would have to pay the brewery, and from then on my grandfather, grandmother, father and mother would be entirely responsible for the success or failure of this business. The previous two years operating as a managed house had given definition to the various roles each would play. Bertie was front of house, the figurehead, he would meet and greet and as mentioned before, was always smartly dressed in his 3 piece suit, white shirt with starched collar, shoes highly polished and a gold pocket watch (which I still have today)with a gold guard tucked in his waistcoat pocket. He would invariably be seen chatting to the customers and generally making them welcome, but when the pub was busy you would find him at the back of the bar as it was all hands to the pumps.

My father was responsible for the day to day running, organising the staff by now numbering 32, both full and part time, cleaners, waiters, barmaids and men, and a full time cellar man. My mother on the other hand ran the home washing and cleaning, cooking for the family and in the evening serving behind the bar. The formidable Florrie however ran the business side handling all the accounts, making up the wages, sorting out the tax and paying all the bills. In the evening usually around 9o'clock she would swan down the central staircase which ran into the hall, after taking her time attending to her appearance, she would make her grand entrance only to spend the rest of the evening chatting to the customers, she was never seen at the back of the bar.

Licensing laws strictly controlled opening hours for licensed premises and varied only slightly between different authorities, the Brown Cow opened weekdays at 10am closed after the lunchtime session at 3pm, opening again at 5.30pm until 10.30pm, but on Sundays lunchtime session hours were 11am until 2pm opening again from 6pm until 10.30pm. This allowed our family to all sit down together to Sunday lunch. My mother would spend Sunday morning preparing and cooking a Sunday roast joint which varied week by week between beef, pork and lamb. The joints supplied by the local butcher would always feed more than we needed and in the case of pork would be a whole leg still on the bone cooked to perfection and would emerge from the huge range with its skin scored to produce delicious crackling, around the meat would be roast potatoes which would have absorbed the fat. The meal started with Yorkshire puddings made in small bun tins which appeared from the range in a constant stream, my father having a dozen to himself but the rest of us could eat our fair share. Accompanying this delicacy would be copious quantities of thick brown onion gravy served in large jugs, there was always a range of pickles, the favourite being sliced raw onion and cucumber sprinkled with sugar and marinated in vinegar. The meat then followed, with whichever sauce was the appropriate accompaniment, homemade mint sauce for the lamb, horseradish sauce for the beef and apple sauce for the pork, with an added item of sage and onion stuffing cooked in small round tins with roast and mashed potatoes, vegetables in season but always mushy peas which had been steeped overnight from the dried pea variety along with a tablet of Bicarbonate of Soda. Sitting down with us on occasions would be Dennis the bar cellar man and Vi the chief barmaid, and at the head of the table Florrie would always carve the joint. Dessert more often than not would be rice pudding which Mother would cook in a large oval Pyrex dish with brown skin and a nutmeg topping and this was served into individual dishes with a dollop of strawberry jam. Wine was never drunk with either dinner or Sunday lunch only becoming popular with working and middle class English in the late sixties, however water, cordial or beer was freely available in our home. My recollection of this regular event is that the meal would be taken in virtual silence punctuated only by the odd request to pass either vegetables or gravy etc. but having eaten our fill, Florrie would then call the meeting to order and heated discussions would take place as to what had gone wrong the preceeding week, and if the arguments appeared to be getting out of hand Florrie would use the handle of the carving knife banged on the table to bring the meeting to order. There was nothing expected from my brother and I except to sit there and suffer in silence, but being old enough to form opinions it seemed to me that Florrie did very little in the way of physical work but seemed to have everybody frightened to death, and it was she who should be obeyed. However expanding that opinion I also realised that this business had to be a way of life requiring a commitment of seven days a week 52 weeks a year leaving very little time for any other interests or hobbies, and I suppose that it is around then that I came to the conclusion that when it became necessary to find my way in life I would avoid like the plague the adoption of the licensed trade as a career.

It is not every Sunday afternoon that the family had a large Sunday lunch, this period of time being the only free time that the licensee gets we would occasionally go visit my paternal grandparents, they lived in a suburb of Leeds called Wortley. I was always pleased to see Grandad and Grandma Cam, and although our visits were infrequent because of dad's commitment to the pub they made us very welcome. Robert was Granddad's Christian name he was a signalman working for British Rail and the signal box he operated was close to his home, and occasionally he would take me to his place of work. It was fascinating how the railway signals were changed to and how much physical effort was required to change them. My brother and I were his only male grandchildren and because I was older he enjoyed time spent with me and took me see his allotment which he was very proud of, and in his spare time produced most of the vegetables that he and my grandmother required. When he retired, he was presented with a gold watch for 45 years service to British Rail North Eastern region, which is engraved with his name along with the details of his service. I was left this watch in his will as I was the only other R Cam in the family, and it is a very treasured possession.

Being a proud Yorkshireman I always hoped that the origin of the name Cam was linked to the Yorkshire Dales, there is a village called Cam, and there is a Cam Fell but this is not the case, my grandfather came to Yorkshire in rather tragic circumstances. Robert was one of four children of Tom and Elizabeth Cam, they lived in the village of Cam in Gloucestershire and unfortunately Tom died in early middle age from a disease related to mining, and being the only breadwinner Elizabeth, who went by the name of Bessie had to find work for her eldest son as there was no welfare state at this time. The work she found was on the railway in Shipley near Bradford which meant she had to bring the family to Yorkshire. Being unable to afford the rent for property close to the station, the nearest rented accommodation she could afford was in Baildon which would mean that Robert had a 2 mile walk to his place of work. Robert's elder sister also found work in the area and Bessie was a herbalist, a skill she had learnt whilst living in Gloucestershire. There being no National Health Service at this time, the local population had to pay to see a doctor. More often than not the poor people would seek a remedy to their ailments from Bessie. She eventually became a legend in the area and took the name Nurse Cam. Robert eventually married Nora Annis and they also set up home in Baildon and subsequently had five children, my father being the eldest boy. On a visit to Baildon with my auntie Muriel and uncle Ernest about ten years ago we happened to meet a lady member of the Antiquarian Society whilst we were looking for the place where my father and his siblings were born. When the lady eventually found out that I was Jack Cam's son she told me she'd been at school with my father and confessed to having a crush on him. Meeting this lady meant I was able to confirm all the facts about my early relations.

Chapter 8

My father up until this point in his life had not found the need for a motor car as he had always used public transport to get to and from work, but with the pub doing well it was agreed he should learn to drive and purchase a motor car. He took a few driving lessons and soon passed his test and the first car he bought was Wolsey which my mother approved of, slightly more upmarket than most vehicles on the road at that time. Dad used it for business collecting small items when we had run out of stock, but as far as he was concerned its major advantage was when he was able to drive to Leeds United football matches, his one indulgence away from work and family, being a keen sportsman in his youth and now an ardent Leeds United fan. He would pick up three of his friends on Saturday afternoon and travel to Leeds United football ground in Elland Road. On one such occasion he was in a traffic jam in York Road parked in this queue of traffic alongside the swimming baths, just where there was what was locally known as a tram pinch where the tramlines came close to the curb and footpath on the nearside of the tram. The driver of a tram proceeding down York Road noticed that there was a queue of stationary traffic, but when he applied the brakes because of steel wheels on steel lines the tram continued through the tram pinch scraping down the side of my father's car taking with it the door handles and causing some superficial damage to the bodywork. I was not party to what took place afterwards but I'm sure the air was blue during my father's conversation with the tram driver, not to mention my mothers conversation with my father when he returned home with the damaged car. I suppose this and similar incidents between trams and the rest of road vehicles left Leeds City Council to abandon the use of trams as a mode of public transport in the city environs. With hindsight and the increasing need of public transport today perhaps Leeds should have kept their trams, as modern designed trams are now in use in major European cities as a very cheap and efficient form of public transport.

Chapter 9

At the age of eleven all schoolchildren were required to take the '11 plus' examination, which if passed allowed them a place at a Grammar School. Failure meant that they would be offered a place at a Secondary Modern school which offered a more skilled base curriculum rather than the more academic path of the Grammar school. This system was changed around the late 50's early 60's as it was thought that the current system of Grammar schools and secondary Modern schools disadvantaged less able children at the age of 11 who might subsequently develop better at a later age. In my opinion the education system that we had at the time of 11plus examinations produced adolescents who would better benefit society by being trained into something that they were capable of doing, and it is a shame that society undervalued skilled based occupations such as carpenters, plumbers, joiners, electricians and engineers, and it is only now that this country lacks such skilled people and are having to import them from such places as Eastern Europe, and that successive Government meddling in the education system has destroyed the best system in the world which existed in the fifties/ sixties. But enough, I will step off my soapbox and continue.

My school reports from Colton County Primary School always included words like caring, considerate, attentive, willing but never included words like clever, I was never near the top of the class in any of the subjects so it came as no surprise that when the results of the 11plus were published I hadn't passed, so a place at the local secondary modern seemed inevitable. However after much deliberation between parents and grandparents it was decided I should take the entrance examination for a small private school near the centre of Leeds. The consideration for this momentous decision was mainly financial as most children who took the entrance exam passed, so it was in September 1954 that I started my further education at City High School for boys and girls in Woodhouse Lane, Leeds. The school was housed in a large terrace opposite the Parkinson Building of Leeds University, the building had been extensively altered to provide a large assembly hall, numerous classrooms all on four floors along with the requisite toilets, offices, staffrooms and storage areas. The school's Headmistress and owner was Muriel Clues the wife of Australian International rugby star Arthur Clues, who was the schools rugby coach and physical education master. A full complement of staff capable of educating children, both boys and girls, in a wide range of subjects up to GCE 'O' level, the standard of teaching and the range offered was good but the task which the staff faced was a difficult one on the basis that their raw material comprised mainly of 11plus failures, whose parents were prepared to pay for their children to improve academically. The next five years at school proved to be a low point in my life, I was a poor pupil, my English was atrocious, and consequently so were other subjects that required written submission. My spelling was and to this day is appalling, and it is only now that I have come to realise that I am slightly dyslexic. I have the classic symptoms of being unable to distinguish between left and right, mixing up when I am writing b's d's p's and q's and it is only recently recognised as an academic disability. In the 50's and 60's my school work in written subjects was affected as I tended to write the first letter and then tail off with some illegible scribble if I was unable to spell a word, which tended to frustrate the teachers marking this work who would invariably strike through it with red ink and mark it down. Nevertheless I excelled in maths and art.

The games facility of the school was good. The Gymnasium was housed in a church hall opposite the school but did not boast machines that Gymnasiums have today, instead had a vaulting horse with springboard, a climbing frame up one wall with ropes and was marked out as a badminton court so physical exercise would be taken twice a week. One of Arthur's favourite exercises was to divide the boys into two teams at each end of the court and throw an eight pound medicine ball over the net, while members of the opposing team had to catch it. For the less muscular members this proved impossible, however one of my schoolmates Roger Cannon, unusual for that day and age, worked out regularly with weights and developed a very muscular physique. He was able to lob the ball extremely high so it was virtually impossible to catch, nevertheless myself being a big lad, this usually ended up being a contest between the two of us. In winter, games such as rugby union for the boys and hockey for the girls would be played on fields on the outskirts of Leeds, and consequently would take up one whole afternoon as travel from school would be involved. Rugby was Arthurs forte, it was his game and he was a great coach. We were taught to play Rugby Union and would be taken to one of three grounds a busride away from school. Arthurs favourite ground was at Kirkstall where there was a scrumming machine, a structural steel frame which incorporated large springs and pads for the front row to put their shoulders against, and the pack was able to practice without there being an opposing team. He was encouraging to all the boys regardless of their physique or ability. His language however was my first introduction to the more colourful aspects of English, whilst practicing kicking expressions like "You couldn't kick an old woman off a jerry" were common, or when tackling he could be heard to shout "Imagine you're pulling a nxxxxr off your Mother," political correctness not being what it is today.

Being big and overweight I was always played at loose head prop forward while Toby Ford slighter in stature played at hooker, and Jimmy Ramsden tall and lanky, tight head prop. Roger Cannon played second row behind Jimmy helping to balance the scrum, the four of us maintained our friendship throughout our school days. To my disappointment I was never good enough or fit enough to make the school team as other attributes apart from weight and the ability to push were required to be good at the game. With Arthur's star reputation in the rugby fraternity he occasionally persuaded other rugby internationals to give coaching sessions, and because of this one or two ex pupils played for Yorkshire.

In the summer girls played netball and the boys played cricket, again at remote locations

The cricket ground was on field which was a tram ride away from school, so immediately after lunch we were dispatched with our cricket kit. For the last part of the journey the tram track ran on a route separated from the main carriageway along the side of the extensive green area known as Soldiers fields, a large green area housing many sports fields, which was part of Roundhay Park, Leeds' largest municipal park. The the nearest stop to our cricket ground was half a mile further on, and boys being boys it seemed great fun to chuck your boots and whites out of the tram window to save carrying it all the way back. Cricket was not Arthurs favourite game but being

Australian he felt he ought to show us Poms how good Australians are, he could certainly whack that little leather ball out of the park whenever he connected with a delivery from one of our best bowlers.

As school days turned into weeks and weeks into years it became obvious that I was run of the mill in most subjects and even poor in a few. Whether this was due to a lack of ability or poor inspirational instruction I have no idea, but I still had ambition, so concentrated on subjects I felt I had ability in. Arts seemed to dominate but I also liked Maths, Algebra and Geometry. At home I developed practical skills and the making of model aeroplanes became my obsession.

Chapter 10

By now at the age of 14 it was assumed that I had enough common sense to be able to conduct my own affairs in my leisure time and as I had been trusted to make my own way to school at the other side of Leeds since the age of 11 I was now allowed to travel at night on public transport, which opened up a new range of activities previously denied such as visiting the cinemas and other schoolfriends houses. As mentioned earlier friendship developed between four friends, myself, Roger Cannon, Toby Ford and Jimmy Ramsden, Jim's parents ran a cafe in York Road, an area of Leeds which had modern factories such as Sumrie's and Burton tailoring. The cafe was successful because in those days few factories provided canteen facilities so it's lunchtime trade was excellent but did not have the need to open in the evening. On occasions when the cafe was closed we four lads formed a card school and although we were well underage, whilst playing cards we indulged in the taking of alcohol, usually cider. I suppose the alcohol that adolescents seem to take these days is that of alcopops but this was not available at the time, nevertheless we felt grown-up drinking cider and playing cards and smoking the odd Woodbine. I suppose it was all part of growing up and in actual fact later on we spent time at Roger Cannon's parents caravan on a permanent site called Long Ashes in Threshfield adjacent to Grassington in the Yorkshire Dales. Here for a few days away from all parental control we did what young teenagers do, walked the hills during the day, and hitched a ride on the narrow gauge railway on the limestone trucks which were carrying quarried material from high in the hills to a larger depot near Grassington where the material would be reloaded onto larger rail trucks and distributed throughout England. And in the evening attempted to be accepted in the local public houses in spite of being underage, and when this was sometimes successful managed to purchase alcohol and take it back to the caravan where we indulged in drinking, smoking and talking of girls. It's occasions such as these that we can look back upon with fond memories at the start of our journey towards adulthood.

Chapter 11

With the pub rapidly gaining a reputation as the 'place to be' business increased, consequently it became obvious that another senior member of staff should be recruited, so a bar-cellar man named Dennis in his late forties maybe early fifties was employed and eventually proved to be the perfect addition to the team. Dennis was an early retired soldier who had gained his experience in the licensed trade after leaving the Army in a very upmarket establishment in Cheshire known as the Bells of Peover. He decided to make the move to Leeds because it was where his grown up family were living, and he stayed with our family business until his eventual retirement. Being ex-Army he had ramrod deportment, about five foot ten in height, a sinewy muscular build, greying hair slicked back, a grey military style moustache and when serving at the back of the bar was always well turned out, shoes polished, clean white shirt and a regimental tie.

Behind the Brown Cow was a busy cattle market, the location of which gave rise to an extension of the licensed opening hours for the Market room only, the room was located at the rear of the building on the ground floor facing the cattle market. Farmers brought their livestock for sale on Market days and were able to avail themselves of this special licensing arrangement.

The cattle Market was still a thriving venture with farms from miles around bringing their livestock for sale by auction. It consisted of five large sheds with pens for various types of livestock, pigs, sheep or cattle and probably covered an area of five acres. In the shed nearest the entrance was a circular auction ring with a rostrum to one side and tiered seating all around allowing the potential bidders a view of the beasts for sale as they were driven into the ring and a view of the bidders from the auctioneers rostrum. The ring was mainly used for the sale of large animals with pigs and sheep auctioned from the pens in which they were housed while the auctioneer moved amongst them. Such a busy place naturally had a spin off for trade for the pub.

On Mondays, market day, the farmers who had brought their livestock to market and completed their sales were able to call in the Market room for refreshments. Catering such as it was consisted of trays of warm pork pies delivered by Cardis a well known pie maker in Leeds city centre. The only accompaniment to this delicacy was bottles of brown HP sauce which Bertie doctored when the bottles were half empty by filling them back up to the top with malt vinegar. On one occasion Dennis the chief barman had served a pie to a hungry farmer who had a new bottle of sauce which required vigorous shaking. He was joined shortly after by a colleague also attending the market. "By gum that pie looks good, think I'll have one" he said. When the pie was delivered and seeing the sauce at the side of his colleagues plate he asked for a bottle. The first farmer had had a new bottle so advised his friend to "give it a good shake," but on this occasion Dennis had passed him one of Bertie's doctored bottles. The vigorous shaking resulted in brown sauce covering pie, plate and the whole of the bar top. Dennis, thinking on his feet, saved Bertie's deception being discovered by saying to the farmer "You should have asked for thick or thin!" "Bloody hell George" he said to his friend "What will they bring out next?" On Market days the Market room was always buzzing.

In spite of strict opening time regulations within the licensing laws there were some occasions when these times could be increased, usually for coming of age parties and wedding receptions, however this invariably involved an appearance in the Magistrates Court by the licensee, who had to explain why the opening times should be varied. The existing extended opening hours came about as there had been a cattle market on this site since 1853, and a public house on the site occupied by the current pub at this major crossroads even longer, and had served the market all those years, so the practice was allowed to continue.

Chapter 12

With Berties licenseeship now entering it's sixth year and he being recognised as a Landlord of some standing he became a member of The Licensed Victuallers Association, and my grandmother Florrie became a member of the Ladies Auxilliary, and it didn't take either of them long to take on the Presidency of the Leeds branch. I have vivid recollections of the pair of them dressed in their finery, Bertie in his black tail coat suit, white shirt and bow tie, wearing his collar of office and Florrie in a long evening gown wearing all her jewellery amongst which was a diamond ring that my wife wears today. They would stop in the public bar for a drink with the customers before the taxi arrived to whisk them off to a hotel venue in the city for a banquet with all the great and good of the City attending. It is only now that I have come to realise my Dads remark to my Mother was not meant as a compliment when he said "She thinks she's the Queen!". Occasionally branch meetings of the Licensed Victuallers and the Ladies Auxilliary would be held in one or others public houses and the Brown Cow suited this purpose admirably as it had a function room on the first floor which was perfect for conducting private business. Florrie on these occasions was in her element, so many years later when I was to join Round Table my mother used to say that I had inherited Florries enjoyment of service in the community.

Jack was heavily involved in the running of the Pub and consequently had little time to spend with his two sons. In fact the business took up most of his time with the exception of one night a week when he took mother out usually to another pub to see how the opposition were doing, much to my Mothers annoyance. This has always formed my opinion that the licensed trade was certainly not to be where my future lay. For my Mother and Father and for Florrie and Betrie their whole lives including social activities revolved around the running of the pub to the exclusion of all else. To be a successful landlord they had to be where the public could see them, and that meant 52 weeks a year 7 days a week, so I suppose because there were four adults involved it did allow for brief holidays. The only other social activity my father took part in, in fact it was his passion verging on obsession, were Saturday afternoons given over to watching Leeds United, he never missed a home game. A season ticket was one of his few extravagancies but funnily enough he never encouraged his two sons. I never attended a game and my brother Michael only once, consequently I had more direction from my mother who did all the parental things like helping with homework, or having some interest in what I was involved with.

Jack was always working but with Sunday opening hours for licensed premises being more restricted it left Sunday afternoons free, and with the business being more successful, my Dad by now being a committed motorist, we would go out as a family to visit my dads relations, his parents, my paternal grandmother and grandfather, who lived in another part of Leeds or one of his two sisters who lived in Doncaster both married to policemen. Nora the eldest with two daughters and Muriel with three daughters. Joyce the youngest sister did not have children and lived in the Pudsey area of Leeds quite close to Dads younger brother Ted who had one daughter. These occasions usually meant tea with tinned salmon, thinly sliced boiled ham and an undressed salad with salad cream on the side and sliced brown bread and butter cut into triangles. The desserts consisted of butterfly buns or jam tarts. I suppose the one exception was when we visited Molly and Ted, my Dads brother and sister in law, her coming from a commercial baking family she would produce beautiful custard tarts, Yorkshire curd tarts and home made iced long buns locally known as Sally Lunns. With such delightful baking it's no wonder I was overweight. These social occasions meant dressing up in Sunday best for Mum and Dad and for Michael and I clean school uniforms and best behaviour to be adhered to at all times.

Chapter 13

Jack for some reason awoke around 2am and decided to investigate the cellar, there was no specific reason for this, his bedroom was a fair distance from the cellar and it was highly unlikely that he would have heard any noise. The only access to the cellar apart from the barrel drop was under the main hall staircase, and at the bottom of the cellar steps to the left was the boiler house which always had its door closed in order to not increase the cellar temperature, however this particular morning the door was slightly ajar. Jack in dressing gown, pyjamas and slippers would be no match for an intruder so looking round he armed himself with a tilting baton, a three foot long 4x2" timber with a T bar at the top and notches along one edge. Its normal use was to tilt the barrel when it was almost empty to extract the last drop. I suppose it never occurred to him that neither dog had been disturbed so the likelihood of it being an intruder was remote.

Suitably armed he slowly pushed open the boiler house door to find a scene he could hardly take in, but there also dressed in night attire was Bertie. He had the door of the boiler open and a large cardboard box full of paper from which he was taking handfuls and throwing it into the furnace. "What are you doing Bert?" "Well Jack you know that the Government are replacing the large white 5pound notes with a smaller bank note and I cannot possibly take this amount of cash to the Bank without an investigation by the Tax Office".

Jack replied "You go to bed and I'll see to this for you".

The next morning I was awakened early by my father. "Come with me".

Leeds Market is something of a landmark, a wonderful stone Gothic facade extremely ornate with much figured stonework, turrets and ornate roof work, it has four entrances one on each corner of the building and in those days had large oak doors and suitably impressive brass door furniture. It was built on the site of the old market in 1857 and once inside, a cast iron structure held up the glazed roof on slender iron columns, this gave a large open space in which market stalls were erected selling mainly foodstuffs, meat, fish, bread, fruit and vegetables and general grocery. In the centre mounted on an ornate iron column is a large 4 faceted clock commemorating one early stall, that of Marks and Spencer's humble beginnings. Along three sides is a high level walkway from which access to the market offices could be gained. Sadly today this is not used, to the East is a further covered area which accommodated more stalls as the market increased in popularity. This area was damaged by fire in 1975 and quickly rebuilt and now even further to the East is an area of open stalls.

Along the West is Vicar Lane, to the South is Kirkgate and to the North is Market Street. This street in 1957 was lined at either side with barrows from which other market traders plied their wares. These were the shadiest characters of all and were known as 'barrow boys' and it is here where Dad and I made several trips with a satchel full of white fivers. He walked down one side of Market Street and I down the other exchanging the fivers for current usable currency. "Don't get less than four quid for each one," he said. Because the barrow boys handled small amounts of cash they were able to still bank these white 5 pound notes for the full value, and this is how we converted Bertie's savings, a practice never to be undertaken again.

Chapter 14

In my early teens I was very overweight and I now think there were two contributory factors, at the age of 5, I contracted scarlet fever and although there is no scientific reason for my assumption I believe it changed the way my metabolism worked, the other factor playing in my lack of weight control was my Mother God Bless her, and because of rationing of eggs, milk and sugar before and just after the war, she fed me large amounts of these foodstuffs including chocolate and sweets. We now know however that foods such as these in anything other than moderation are bad for you, and cause many of the problems that my generation suffer from today, such as heart disease and diabetes. I was a 'fat kid' and as a consequence of this found it difficult to relate to the opposite sex. So as mentioned earlier, it was no wonder that my attention was drawn to model aeroplane building, with Balsa wood tissue paper and dope and with a rubber band motor I created some stunning models, only to be heartbroken when they crashed usually after only a few flights. The hobby took on a new direction entirely with the purchase of a small diesel engine, but the technical advanced radio control had not yet been developed so a control line was the most popular way, with the model aircraft connected by two control lines which offered up and down movement while flying in a circle. These small diesel engines had to be started by flicking the propeller with two fingers and if the operator was not quick enough when the engine started it usually resulted in damaged digits. Balsa wood, tissue paper and glue were the basic construction materials, plans and the materials could be purchase separately but the most common way was to buy a Kielkraft kit which came with everything required for the finished model.

However with hormonal changes taking place curiosity still existed, and it was not long before an opportunity presented itself. Just along Colton Road there was a fork where the left hand continued on to Colton and the right hand was a gated carriage drive to Templenewsam. The gates were painted white and just in front was a long bench, and this was the place where early secondary education children, both girls and boys, liked to congregate away from grown ups where they could try the odd fag and other forbidden pursuits. As the adventures progressed we found an even more secure place well out of the way. Just below the news agents at the corner of Colton Road there was a farmyard, and apart from the farmhouse it had many outbuildings, stables and the like and a large barn with an enormous door opening on to Colton Road high enough to allow access to hay wagons. Cut into this door was a small personal access door which was never locked, and it was through there that we kids were able to gain access to a barn full of hay and straw, and so, not making any noise to attract attention it was in such an environment that "you show me yours and I'll show you mine" was our first introduction to the difference. Another occasion when I was left alone with a girl of my own age was when my cousins were visiting with my aunt and uncle from Doncaster, and while the grown ups were catching up with what was happening in their lives, we were exploring our differences in the potting shed in the garden. All this happened in my early teens and it seems a shame nowadays that the age of innocence, because of Information Technology, has been drastically reduced.

Chapter 15

Cellar work, and in particular looking after cask conditioned beers, required particular skills. The beer was delivered in wooden casks and would still carry some of the sediment which was naturally disturbed in the delivery process, therefore careful conditioning was necessary before the beer could be sold. It was CAMRA that coined the phrase "Real Ale" which has had such a resurgence in modern times. The involved process of keeping beer at the "Fisherman's Hut" still applied to the Brown Cow with one notable difference, the deliveries to the Brown Cow were in Hogsheads, the largest of all the barrel sizes containing 54 gallons, and were extremely heavy, and because of the pubs location were delivered on a wagon and not a Dray, and the skill of the men delivering it still known as Draymen was most impressive, spinning a hogshead off the wagon onto a padded sack and then down the beer shute and onto the gantry. Once the barrel was on the gantry it became Dennis's responsibility, a large bung was left at the lowest point as the barrel lay horizontally on the gantry, through which Dennis had to drive a tap very quickly so as not to spill any of the contents. On the top of the barrel was another smaller bung into which either a hardwood plug or a cane plug would be driven, depending on how much air was required inside the barrel. Through this bung, finings (egg albumen supplied by brewing suppliers Gaskell and Chambers) were introduced through a large brass pump instrument. This procedure was necessary to settle the sediment after delivery. Dennis's responsibility was also to draw off as much of the sediment as possible when the barrel was almost empty and introduce it back into the next barrel to be used, through a large brass and copper funnel lined with a filter paper. This practice had to be carried out in order to maximise the quantity of beer to be sold.

The weekends were becoming particularly busy and on Sundays the whole of the 32 staff both full and part-time would be employed. Strict opening times were observed but it appeared that a bus would arrive at the stop outside the Brown Cow just before opening time. Bertie would stand in the centre of the hall with a gold pocket watch in hand waiting for midday when he could give the signal to the waiters attending all three entrances to open. The bar staff would be employed half an hour early in order to draw pints of bitter, mild, leaving just enough to top them up when they were required. These pints were placed a large trays holding 20 at a time and at the signal from my grandfather the doors would open and a surge of customers would surge through.

The partly filled pints will be topped up and the waiters dressed in white jackets served each separate room. Waiter service was the norm in large pubs around this time. If a customer required a pint of mixed at opening times he had to wait as the aforementioned practice could not be applied.

Chapter 16

One day when I was at school the headmistress called me out to tell me that there had been a message from my mother informing me that my grandmother had had a heart attack and was gravely ill and had been taken to hospital. When I arrived home from school there was only my dad in left to run the pub as my mum and grandfather had gone to the hospital to be by my grandmother's side. Later that evening when Mum and Bert returned from hospital I learned that my grandmother had passed away and both Mum and Bert was terribly upset.

The funeral took place five days later and the service was held at Whitkirk church, the church immediately opposite the pub. She was interred in the cemetery 400 yards further down Selby road. It was attended by many people, a large number of my grandmother and grandfather's relations, customers, and a director of Tetleys demonstrating the high regard that the brewery held for my grandparents.

My mother had laid on a funeral tea in the banqueting room on the first floor of the Brown Cow to which most of the mourners attended.

Florrie my grandmother was a formidable character and a major part of the team that ran the Brown Cow, but the work she did still had to be done so it was split between Dad and Bertie.

Most schools at this time organised a school trip during the summer holidays and the City High School was no exception, and the trip was organised to spend a week in Grasse in southern France. It was open to all those pupils that were in their last year of secondary education before they went on to take A-levels or employment. Most of the students of that year took the opportunity to join the trip. Travelling involved a train journey to London King's Cross station, a train to Calais, then on to Paris and an overnight sleeper train to Aix- en -Provence and a bus to Grasse. Although the journey took a day and a half our spirits were high because for most of us continental journey was a new experience. When we eventually got on the sleeper train it was evident that the school plus Masters would take up one complete carriage leaving two pupils to spend the night in a another compartment in another carriage. The master in charge chose Roger Cannon and I to spend the night away from the rest of the group as in his opinion, we seemed more sensible than the rest. The compartment had six bunks three on each side already made up with blankets and pillows and as there was no one about Roger and I chose the top two bunks, shortly afterwards a young couple came in and after undressing down to their underwear chose the middle two bunks. The last to arrive were two middle-aged men and after taking off their jackets one took his shoulder holster and gun off and hung it on the peg provided. This scary experience for two teenagers was really out of the ordinary, but for me this monumental journey had another incident in store. The train made a stop in Lyon, I assume to change drivers, and just about this time I needed a pee, but I found the doors in the carriage were locked and I didn't have access to the toilet, so I got off the train to get back on a carriage which had toilet. This partially undressed youth walking about the platform in stocking in feet alerted a guard who immediately came up to me and spoke to me in French, I tried to explain in what knowledge of my French language was that I needed the toilet, we eventually made each other understand using pidgeon French and English that I had to get back on the carriage where my compartment was as the practice of locking carriage doors was to stop robbers running through the train, and that once the train was in motion the doors would be unlocked. At around 8 am we were offered breakfast of croissant and coffee after which we were able to relate our story to one of the masters. A bus journey from Aix to Grasse completed the journey when we arrived at the school where we were to spend our holiday. For most of us experiencing another country's culture was certainly an eye-opener, and one of the major differences was the toilet, which was a small room with two handles on the wall at either side of a hole in the floor. I now understand that French plumbing has been updated!.

The weather, the food and the whole experience I, like most of the others thoroughly enjoyed, and it gave me an interest in foreign travel when much later on, married and with children we spent lots of holidays travelling through France.

I was always tall for my age and consequently was soon to be employed in the family business in my spare time, so at around the age of 16 when Dad was short staffed I was asked to serve behind the bar of the taproom, the regular barman of the taproom was Alf a congenial sort of chap probably in his early 50s who got on well with the regular customers who liked to drink in the taproom. Here was a place where workmen could wind down from their busy day, a place where they didn't have to change their clothes, a place where they could escape from their womenfolk, a place where they could indulge in the usual pub games such as dominoes and darts. The drinks that were served in the taproom were usually pints of beer either bitter or mild or mixed, it was very rare that any other alcoholic drinks were sold. When I first started serving I was shown how to pull a pint with the hand pulled beer engine so that it finished up with about half an inch of creamy head on the top and I recall the cost of these drinks was a shilling for a pint of bitter,10d for a pint of mild and 11d for a pint of mixed, a shilling equates to 5p in today's currency with the 10d and 11d being proportionately less. The taproom was a place for men only, the place which women didn't frequent and consequently the language was colourful, it was a place where politics were discussed, a place where a man could argue his point, there was rarely any trouble but occasionally men being men and the prevalence of alcohol trouble flared up. My Dad had a way of dealing with such situations and I recall being present on one occasion when one of the customers had to be removed as he had had too much drink and was causing offence. Alf called my father who was serving at another bar but came straight away to sort out the problem. It was fairly obvious that the man was causing a commotion and as soon as Dad appeared the customer became violent. Dad went round the other side of the bar, removed his spectacles and said to the man "Come outside". Dad led the way and as soon as the man was halfway through the door my father rammed it in the man's face, this immediately defused the situation and the man went home with a sore head. "You see" Dad said to me "This practice is all part of being a landlord".

Chapter 17

At the age of 16 it became obvious that I was not sufficiently academic to pursue a further education taking A-levels and then following on to University, in fact in those days only 4% of school leavers went on to pursue a University education so it seems that the correct course of action would be that I should seek employment in an industry that would offer part-time further education. With my 4 'O' levels, mathematics, art, and to my surprise English literature, and English-language, I had no idea of the type of work to which I would be suited. My father however had decided the direction my career should take and had arranged that I should attend an interview for position of a Junior engineer with a company called Pavior Construction Company in Shipley, this interview did actually take place within a week of my leaving school.

It was on a Saturday morning in early September 1959 that I found myself at a desk in the managing director's office working through mathematical problems that Jack Kenyon the MD had set for me. That day and the outcome of that interview proved to be the most defining moment of my future in the world of work and in fact of my life as a whole, as it meant that I embarked on a career that I was entirely happy with and formed the basis of financial stability which allowed me to bring up a family and even today would be regarded by most people as having a comfortable life. I had very little knowledge of civil engineering but had noticed while cycling around the area in which we lived or walking the dog in the more remote parts, there were construction sites which had a compound and temporary offices and I thought then that this would be a nice place to work. It must have been a Saturday morning when Jack Kenyon had little to do as the interview lasted two hours, and at the end of which I was offered the job of Junior Engineer at a salary of £2.10 shillings a week for a 4 ½ day week to include a Saturday morning and one day to attend college, firstly to obtain an Ordinary National Certificate in building and secondly to obtain a Higher National Certificate in Civil Engineering. I was to report to the drawing office located on the first floor of the head office in Shipley at 9 am the following Monday morning, and after a period of introduction to the various engineers seated at drawing boards (an environment in which I felt perfectly comfortable) I was under Jack Kenyon's instructions to demonstrate some initiative. I had to sort out employment records from the company's tax office which was located in Bradford City Centre.

Although up to this point I had lived in Leeds, I had never visited the centre of its adjacent city, Bradford. So after

catching the bus on that Monday morning from Shipley to
Bradford and arriving in this wonderful stone city in 1959
I was immediately blown away by the magnificence of the
city centre buildings. The development of such a place
was made on the back of the wool trade which attracted
many entrepreneurs who made vast fortunes but chose
to spend some of their wealth in the construction of the
beautiful buildings which I then found myself surrounded
by. I did quite quickly find the tax office responsible for
the affairs of Pavior Construction Company and availed
myself of the required employment records, but before
returning to Shipley I spent a little time wandering around
Bradford City centre. Tragically within a year of my initial
introduction to Bradford the heart of it was ripped out
and replaced by reinforced concrete monstrosities under
the guise of modern redevelopment overseen by one all-
powerful bureaucrat, the Borough Engineer.

I was to spend the first two months of my employment
with Pavior Construction Company in the drawing
office of the head office, being a general factotum filing
documents, fetching and carrying for the engineers within
the drawing office, and occasionally going out on site
with one or other of the engineers. While some work
carried out in the drawing office was for the bigger sites
the majority of work undertaken from this office were
for those of a small nature who didn't require permanent
on site management and would probably only last two or

three weeks, nevertheless it was all part of my introduction to Civil Engineering.

One section of the company specialised in surface dressing, a form of maintenance surfacing to carriageways which was carried out by spraying hot bitumen from a tanker onto the existing carriageway and then spreading clean chippings, usually Granite, onto the hot bitumen. This was then rolled and after a couple of days the loose material that was not bedded into the bitumen would be brushed up. It is a quick and easy surface and can be applied to many miles during a day.

The engineer in charge of this work was John Swales and I would accompany him on his trips out to meet with the local authority engineer for whom we were carrying out this work to measure and agree the work done and produce an account for payment. Because of the large areas covered it was to be found more prudent to measure the length of carriageway surfaced with a measuring wheel. I would sit in the boot of John Swales car holding the measuring wheel on the road while John and the local authority engineer would sit in the car and drive over the work done, occasionally stopping to take a width measurement.

After this initial 3 months office period I was told I was to report to the site office on the Micklefield bypass A1M construction site the following Monday morning at 8 am. This move was to give me further grounding in the type of work that a civil engineering company would carry out.

The works compound was situated in Station Yard which was comprised of a collection of wooden huts. In the centre of the compound was the agents office, the term agent refers to the company representative on site, the man in charge of the whole operation and had the responsibility of the whole of the works, the employment of the necessary staff, the engagement of the necessary machines and the various subcontractors. Needless to say on a large construction site most of these responsibilities were delegated to other staff who were located in other offices around the compound. There was one for the site clerk who dealt with the financial running of the site including payment of the staff. There was one for the engineers (the place which I became familiar with as this was my initial introduction to the world of work). There was also a canteen and kitchen which produced meals for the workforce at break times. This facility which was available to all could only be taken up by those working close because this particular contract covered a distance of approximately 5 miles, so a large amount of the workforce breaks had to be taken where they were working. There was also a small office for the general foreman, a man who in most people's opinion ran the site, I was later to realise after working on many large civil engineering projects that the general foreman would be invaluable. Most were hard men who had worked their way up through the ranks within the construction industry and because of their previous experience had earned the respect that was necessary to motivate a large labour force made up mainly of men used to working in all weather conditions and in difficult environments. The rest of the buildings within the compound were mainly for the storage of materials used in construction which were vulnerable to either the ravages of the weather or of pilfering.

Fortunately the location of the site compound was adjacent to a railway station and I was able to catch a train from Crossgates, a station to which I could walk from the Brown Cow (a distance of approximately ¾ of a mile) and because of the trains time of arrival at Micklefield station just before 8 am, I was able to get to work on time.

I was assigned to the site engineers who had an office entirely to themselves. There was a chief engineer Jim Clapham, a senior engineer Barry Marley, Alf Feather the setting out engineer and me who was on probation to see whether I suited the firm and the job suited me. From day one there was no doubt in my mind that this was to be my chosen vocation, I loved every aspect of it. Everyone employed on this site was there to create a new motorway, a functional thing and a necessary thing that provided rapid transport for goods materials, and the general opinion was that it would create wealth for the economy of the country, nevertheless in my opinion was a thing of beauty. Even during its construction it gave rise to spectacular events such as the movement of vast quantities of earth and operations carried out by huge machines. The operation called 'cut and fill' removed material from high ground and deposited it in the low ground thus levelling out the route the motorway was to take. I was extremely impressed when I witnessed the power of the machines engaged in this work, a large caterpillar bulldozer designated the D9 had two steal teeth attached to the rear of the machine which was hydraulically forced into the ground, in this case limestone rock, the machine was then driven forward ripping up large quantities of material. At the front of this bulldozer was a small blade. This engaged the rear of another machine also built by Caterpillar named the DW 21, its job was to lower the underside of the body also having a blade which when forced forward would scoop up this loose material and when full of at least 25ton would lift up the body and drive away on its huge pneumatic tyres and deposit the material in layers in the areas of fill and the material would be compacted with an enormous vibrator roller. The engineers would carry out tests to ascertain whether the compact was sufficient to avoid subsidence when the motorway was completed. As this work was being carried out 24 hours a day, I was able to see from the train on my way to work that the areas of the low ground was growing daily. Also I was able to witness the construction of bridges(to take the motorway over or under existing roads and railways) and culverts (to take the groundwater and existing watercourses under the new road). I quickly realised that everyone had a part to play and even me in my lowly role as chain man (someone who anchors the non-intelligent end of a measuring tape from given points to allow the engineer to locate the true line of the new motorway). I enjoyed the camaraderie which existed between all the labour force, I enjoyed the fact that most of my work was to be undertaken outdoors, but I also enjoyed the aspect of work which required me to be in doors plotting information gleaned outside, and using my mathematical knowledge to compute volumes of materials used which in turn could become introduced into a bill of quantities for work done on a monthly basis, and submitted for payment by the authority whose job it was to provide the motorway.

Chapter 18

By now **Bertie** had been a tenant landlord of the Brown cow for approximately 8 years and as the business was doing well it was decided that he and my father should have new motor cars, Bertie favoured a new black Ford Zephyr Zodiac automatic being the vehicle with the most advanced technology. Jack on the other hand decided on a Vauxhall Cresta a car designed by Americans with masses of chrome and fins to the rear, it was painted in two tone light green and cream (mother loved it). At the same time I had become eligible to drive and it was decided I should take a course of lessons with a local driving school. The first vehicle on which I learned to drive was a Morris Minor, the four-speed manual gearbox was most forgiving and was the vehicle of choice at that time for people to learn on. Like most 17 year olds at the time I loved the motor car and was desperate to have a driving licence and to be able to drive without adult supervision and be free to go where I liked, so in my haste to pass my test and my over confident attitude to my driving ability I was entered for my driving test after six lessons I was soon brought down back to earth by my failure to pass on this early attempt. However I immediately made reapplication and was fortunate to pass on my second attempt. The responsibility of having under my control what is ostensibly a lethal weapon was brought sharply into focus on the occasion of my first opportunity of driving my father's new Cresta without supervision. One Saturday morning I was allowed to take the car to work whilst working on the Micklefield bypass, it was a great opportunity to be able to show off and as I drove into the compound in station yard a little boy from one of the terrace houses above ran towards me, I felt and heard a bang and all my worst fears immediately took over. After the initial shock I was able to get out of the car and run round to the nearside and to my great relief found the little boy sat on the ground apparently unhurt, in his excitement at seeing the car he had run into it. Incidents such as that makes all newly qualified drivers very aware of what they have at their control. After dusting the lad down and making sure he was unhurt I was able to park the car and show it off to the rest of the engineering team on site.

My grandfather as mentioned earlier was a motoring enthusiast and in the days when very few motorcars were on the road he would be one of the first in Leeds to own one, so with that in mind and with his grandson newly qualified as a licensed driver he decided he would purchase my first car. Bertie decided that we ought to look at a sports car and I ended up with a second-hand MG TC. though I didn't realise it at the time there were very few 17 year olds able to own and drive such an iconic vehicle. This development could reduce my journey time considerably and also when I owned independent means of transport should I have to go on errands for the company they paid me a mileage allowance. I have always realised how extremely fortunate I was to be able to own and afford a motor car and even doubly fortunate that the car Bertie chose was a second-hand MG TC sports car. How he managed to obtain insurance for such a vehicle for such an inexperienced driver still remains a mystery.

So for the short period of time left for my employment on the Micklefield bypass I was able to travel in style. However we very quickly realised that the TC engine was not the most reliable and we were able to do a deal with the second hand sports car specialists that supplied the vehicle in the first place to upgrade it to a MG TF a vehicle even more ostentatious.

I quickly learned what would be required of me as a site engineer and with the pressure of work increasing with the pace of construction I was soon allowed the responsibility of the use of the Theodolite and Level and the setting out of various aspects of the work. Because of the increasing responsibility placed upon me it was obvious that the engineers required another chain man and one of the site labourers known as Ginge, for his mop of ginger hair, was to work with the engineers as chain man and to assist with the mixing of concrete to secure setting out. Ginge would work with Alf and myself as we set out pegs and profiles for the machinery to work to, these guidelines usually made of wood would require concreting in so that accidental knocks wouldn't move them off-line. To assist us in this work we were given the use of an old Bedford van which had been part of a fleet of vehicles owned by the Bradford Dyers Association, (Pavior Construction's parent company) which we used to transport our setting out equipment, the various instruments, pegs, timber for profiles and small quantities of concrete. The work was never without its humorous side and on occasions when there were no large quantities of concrete being mixed by the on-site batching plant we had to mix our own. This usually meant taking small quantities of sand and gravel into a pile on a board along with some cement taken from a large cement silo. This silo discharged cement through a flexible trunk- like hose clamped shut by two spring-loaded rollers operated by a lever, when the silo was full, a gentle pressure was all that was needed to allow a small quantity of cement to be discharged into a bucket held by someone underneath the hose. However, if the silo was nearing empty it required much more force to be applied to the lever to get even the smallest quantity of cement. On one particular occasion we had to mix concrete and it was obvious that the silo was nearing empty, and a good pressure was required to extract the cement. The day after, we also needed concrete, and having got the required amount of sand and gravel onto the board I asked Ginger to stand with a bucket underneath the trunk, and realising that effort was required yesterday I applied the same amount of effort to the lever, only to discover that there had been a delivery the day before, and a vast pile of cement emerged from the trunk covering Ginger from head to foot. This action made him furious, and he proceeded to chase me up the railway line at the side of the batching plant using as many expletives has he could muster.

As the construction progressed it became obvious that the project was going to be a financial success for the company and consequently certain items of plant were being replaced. One of those items relegated to the scrap heap was our Bedford van to be replaced by a Land Rover with a canvas back. This vehicle made it easier to access the various parts of the site which were still under construction and required an all-terrain vehicle to get to. However I often found other uses for the little vehicle and on one occasion shortly before Christmas Alf and I borrowed a chainsaw and took the Land Rover into a nearby copse where there was a holly tree full of red berries, and it didn't take long to cut the tree down and to chop it into sizeable pieces that we could put in the back of the Land Rover. On returning to the highway we noticed we were being followed by a police car, the policeman had obviously noted that there were bits of holly tree sticking out from under the canvas, so we decided that evasive action should be taken and consequently drove down the new carriageway where the police car couldn't follow us to a manhole which was located in the area still under construction. After removing the manhole lid we pushed our ill-gotten gains down the manhole from which we would be able to retrieve at a later date, after sweeping the back of the Land Rover clean of all evidence, we proceeded into the compound only to find that the police car was there before us and the police officers were being entertained by the site agent. On arrival we were summoned into the agents office only to be confronted by the police who asked if we knew anything about the removal of a holly tree from an estate close by, naturally we denied all knowledge. The police's response to this denial was to issue us with a formal warning that it is an offence to remove trees from other people's land. As soon as the police had driven out of the compound Mr Crow our site agent said" I don't believe your story, what have you done with the holly tree"? We came clean and told him where the fruits of our illegal activity were. His response was for us to retrieve the holly and take it down to Leeds market, sell it to a market trader for what we could, bring back the proceeds and the site staff would all go to the pub that night. Needless to say this episode left Alf and I with a lesson learned.

Chapter 19

It was in the taproom at around this time I used to congregate with a group of lads most of whom had been friends from Scouts or the choir. There was Charlie of course, and there was Alan Wormald a young man who along with his brother ran a garage and workshop in Leeds. He had the use of a Trojan van, the type that was seen in a popular advert of the day which featured a group of chimpanzees delivering, brewing, and drinking tea, it was an advert for PG tips so consequently the van was nicknamed the monkey van. The numbers of those who used to congregate for a night out fluctuated, nevertheless it was usually made up of others such as cousin Chris Mabbot, David Marsden, John Abrams, Harold Abbot, Malcolm Turnbull, Ian Firth, and David Parkin. It was usually a Saturday night when these outings were proposed and a destination was selected some distance away from the Brown Cow where there would be a dance. A designated driver who in spite of the relaxed drink driving laws would not drink on such occasions, but the rest of us would have a half in every hostelry between the Brown Cow and the destination. On arrival at the dance it would be a free for all and for those lucky enough to pull a girl, the van would be available for kissing, while the rest of us carried on drinking. Not always did the group seek a dance hall and instead would drive to another pub. Occasionally the pub chosen would have a stage and a microphone and because of this Charlie couldn't resist getting up on stage and much to the rest of the group's embarrassment he would sing popular songs to anyone who cared to listen. It was obvious that the enjoyment he had as a member of the church choir never left him and much later on he joined a male voice choir. These get togethers continued until my parents eventually left the Brown Cow.

University was only available to 4% of young people interested in taking up further education, consequently selection was made at the age of 16 for those expected to achieve university entrance and continue their education to A level. The other 96% of school leavers in which I was included were encouraged to take further education at a technical college attending night school and possibly one day a week. It was not therefore unusual that the lads I mentioned meeting in the taproom of a Saturday evening did not go on to university but most of them pursued further education in their selected occupations, this meant that not everyone of the group would make every Saturday meeting as their work commitments meant them working away from home.

The group was always good-natured and up for a laugh and intent on having a good night out. Now when most of us had achieved our late teens it was obvious that our characters were formed and such diversity always made for an interesting night. Harold Abbott, always the Joker, made up nicknames for every member, I remember mine being ' pomp man, as I had taken to wearing string vests beneath my shirt and being tall gave a superior impression. Harold did make names for everyone in the group but the one that sticks out in my mind was the one he devised for David Parkin. David worked on the construction of a new bank being built in Garforth (he was an apprentice joiner), and before the bank building was complete during a storm the roof on which David had been working was blown away, this occurrence made the local news and ever since then David's nickname was the' prank manager.'

Harold at the age of 16 had a motorcycle and unfortunately was involved in a serious accident which from his injuries resulted in one of his legs being amputated just below the knee, however this injury did not curtail his enthusiasm for enjoying himself, he was always the life and soul of the group.

Harold, my cousin Chris Mabbot and I had a boating holiday together on the Thames, fortunately the week that we hired the boat the weather was glorious and we were able to swim in the river most days. On one particular occasion Harold had omitted to remove his false leg and as it filled up with water, was dragging him below the surface, he quickly detached the false limb and we were able to dive to retrieve the saturated prosthesis and bring it to the surface. The boat at this time was moored on the riverbank with a well used footpath running past, and the sight of Harold's leg hanging up to dry alongside the three of us sunbathing, caused great mirth amongst the walkers passing this scene. Harold's sense of humour and his propensity to nickname people became part of the eulogy given by the vicar at Harolds premature funeral. Harold passed away in his late 50s, presumably from injuries sustained in that motorcycle accident that none of us realised the severity of, nevertheless most of us were able to attend the funeral service. The vicar who was well known to Harold was also a motorcycle enthusiast, and referred to Harold's many friends by their nicknames including that of the motorcycling vicar (The revved up Rev.)

Chapter 20

As the roadworks progressed on the Micklefield bypass most of the large earthmoving equipment had been moved from site as the cut and fill operation was complete and the nature of the work changed to the provision of edge restraints which would hold the carriageway construction and the inclusion of drainage which would collect the surface water from the final surface of the carriageway. This drainage system known as French drain consisted of a semi-porous pipe laid at approximately a metre deep covered with a gravel filter media which discharged into a catch pit located at the low points of the carriageway, this catch pit in turn would be connected to a drainage system which discharged into the natural watercourses. I have gone into the details of the construction of this drainage system to emphasise what follows.

While excavations for these French drains were being carried out on our site usually by the mechanical excavator which was used at that time, manufactured by well-known manufacturers such as Smith and Ruston Busirus. This type of excavator depended on the weight of the digging bucket attached to an even weightier arm which was drawn in by a system of ropes and pulleys, the whole machine mounted on a large turntable mounted on caterpillar tracks reminiscent of the undercarriage of a tank. The weight of such a machine required large low loaders to transport the same machine to various sites.

So it was with some hilarity amongst the officionados of mechanical excavation that when a Fordson Major tractor arrived on site attached to which seemed to be some Meccano type contraption with a digging bucket at the end all operated by hydraulic rams. It had come to demonstrate its digging ability and was to be set up in competition with one of the standard heavy excavators at either side of a carriageway to excavate the French drain. This test was set up as the excavated depth would be the same at either side of the carriageway. At one side was a Smith 10 the excavator most commonly used for this type of work throughout the world and at the other side was this Fordson Major tractor with the Heath Robinson arrangement attached to its rear. Amongst the old hand construction workers the consensus of opinion was that there was no contest and the old Smith 10 would demonstrate its supremacy, consequently bets amongst the men was inevitable and substantial amounts of money exchange hands. In the event this flimsy arrangement on the back of the tractor completed its length of trench in half the time that the Smith 10 took. At this point I have to say that the driver of that Fordson Major tractor was one Noel Hooper who was employee number one for Mr James Bamford, it never ceases to amaze me that none of the large excavation machinery representatives who were in attendance at this demonstration did not see what the future held, and continued to manufacture the large heavy and expensive machinery until in not many years in the future their businesses failed and JCB became a world leader in the manufacture of construction equipment.

After my initial introduction to civil engineering giving me first-hand experience on a large motorway construction site, I was transferred to head office so I was given the opportunity to see how the administration side of civil engineering works was undertaken. The offices were located in a large two-storey house with a car park at one side and a yard at the other with various industrial sheds which would house plant and equipment. The ground floor offices had a receptionist telephonist, the managing director's office, the managing director's personal assistant office and a communal administrative office, and the accountants office. On the first floor was a large communal engineers office, a separate office housing surfacing and surface dressing management, an estimator's office, and the buyer's office.

Now working in head office I was assigned to the engineers, my job consisted of generally assisting the engineers of which there were five, making the tea, filing documents and drawings and being the general factotum.

The engineering department's responsibility was to carry out some design work where design and construction was required, but their work mainly consisted of working on preprepared schemes submitted by local authorities for open tender. They were also responsible for the measurement of works and submitting these measurements to the estimating department or the accounts department, who in turn would formulate either an estimate or a bill to the authority requiring the work.

There was an intercom telephone system throughout the offices which had a more insistent ring when it was Jack Kenyon the managing director, and it was usually my job to answer the intercom when it was the MD. There was a push button system at the side of the managing directors door which when pressed would indicate, by an illuminated sign whether you had to wait or enter .

It was on one such occasion that I was standing outside the MDs door when the light flashed for me to enter. Kenyon, sitting behind his large desk with 2 well-dressed men at the other side. One of the pieces of furniture in Kenyon's office was a cocktail cabinet and I was asked by Kenyon to ask the two visitors if they would like some refreshment. I asked them what they would like and was informed that whisky was the preferred beverage, and consequently I poured two large shots into 2 separate glasses and and placed them in front of each of the visitors who asked if they could have water with their drink. I left the office for the kitchen to get a jug of water and on my return I leant over the 2 men with the jug in one hand and managed to tip some of its contents onto one of the visitors who immediately leapt up as he realised it was boiling water. Kenyon said "My God lad, I thought you were a landlord's son and should know better that cold water is better in neat whisky".

"Sorry Mr. Kenyon" I replied "I didn't know whether they were Irish or American!". When eventually we had dried off the visitor and things had returned to normal I was introduced to the 2 men, one Peter Bolton and one Ian Appleyard. both principles of major motor retail outlets in Leeds. They were discussing with Kenyon entry to the Tulip Rally, a famous continental motoring competition, and it soon became obvious it was my job for the next week to take away the entry information and work out detailed routes between the various checkpoints. All of this of course was nothing to do with the civil engineering business, but then as long as Kenyon was turning a profit for the company he could do what he liked.

Chapter 21

My **first two** years of employment with Pavior Construction Company made me realise that I had found my true vocation and along with my day release and my evening classes at Bradford College my knowledge of the business that I have come to love increased. In that time I had completed and passed my ordinary national certificate in building construction and went on to study civil engineering at Bradford College of advanced technology which involved the same time commitment as I had at Bradford College i.e. three evening classes a week and one full day, working the other four and a half days for Pavior Construction Company.

As I was now based in Saltaire I decided as an inexperienced driver I would leave the car at home and make the journey to work which was fairly complicated from Whitkirk. I had to walk to the station in Crossgates, catch a train to Leeds then change catch a train to Shipley and then walk from Shipley station to Saltaire Road where the office was located, all of which meant travelling time of an hour and a half each way. Needless to say it was not very long before I decided that the journey times could be drastically reduced if I drove to work in Shipley.

The powers that be decided that my time would be more valuable to me and to the company if I gained experience now in other departments of the company so I fitted in to working in head office very well and soon became familiar with all the members of staff,

Around this time, Jack Kenyon's son Nigel came to be employed by the company and while his father more often than not went into the office each morning he refused to take his son to work. As the Kenyon home was in Roundhay and it was on my way to work I elected to pick Nigel up each morning. Also around this time, Jack Kenyon purchased a Sunbeam Alpine sports car which he occasionally used for work. On one particular morning I had picked up Nigel after his father had already left for work. We both agreed that we should try to get there before he did and save the embarrassment of being hauled over the coals for being late to work. At a distance of approximately 3 miles to the office I managed to catch up Jack and eventually overtake him and therefore was there before he was. Not long after I had arrived in the drawing office, the intercom rang and I was summoned to Kenyon's office. I was informed that I had no longer to transport Nigel to work and that furthermore he would be contacting my father and telling him what a reckless individual I was, and that in his opinion I was not safe on the public highway. Needless to say he was just peeved that I had beaten him to work and the incident was never referred to again.

I loved the MG sports car which for an 18-year-old was the ultimate mode of transport, I suppose this was the start of my major interest in motorcars but I never realised at the time how lucky I was to own a sports car. I regularly polished its gleaming red paintwork and chrome embellishments and carefully looked after the interior which had red leather seats, and red leather facings to the doors and the three octagonal dials on the dashboard. I quickly learnt to service the vehicle and to carry out minor repairs, it really was my pride and joy and I was often seen driving around the area with my best friend Flash the Alsatian in the passenger seat.

My civil engineering course at Bradford's College of Advanced Technology was a large commitment with a day release and three nights, along with plenty of home work in between left me with very little leisure time.

On the nights when it was my night school there was no point in my returning home, so I stayed back after work in the office doing my homework before leaving for the college in Bradford.

It was on one such occasion that I was in the drawing office completing my homework after everyone had gone home before leaving for college, when I heard a noise from a downstairs office. I walked to the top of the stairs to be confronted by a naked woman whom I recognised as the local policewoman hotly pursued by a naked Director

"What the hell are you doing still here Cam" he said. "Doing my homework" I replied," and I see you are doing the same!"

The head office gave me the opportunity to be involved in all aspects of contracting, as mentioned earlier .

Other departments required for the administration of a medium-sized construction company included finance department, purchasing department, small Works Administration Department, and Estimating. There was also a typing pool in an office of their own housing two junior typists, three senior typists and the comptometer operator(this machine a forerunner of a computer was really a glorified calculator but a very necessary piece of equipment and required a skilled operator to use it). Apart from the largest office in the building, that of the Managing Director there was the smallest office in the building, and I had a regular conversation with the telephonist who operated a plug-in switchboard. Beryl [that was her name] was the fount of all knowledge and knew most of what was going on in all departments so she was able to give me an advance notice of which direction the company was moving in. Information I found invaluable assisting me in pursuing my career within the company.

Beryl was in a perfect position to gain all the gossip within the firm so whenever I had the opportunity I would find out from Beryl what was happening with the staff.

After my spell of working in the drawing office I was

to gain experience of the small works department, housed in its own office on the first floor. It had two permanent employees Frank Clare and Jerry Lee, both responsible for the estimating and organising the plant and materials required to carry out the small works. It also had a roving engineer, one Charles Clifton who spent most of his time out of the office either measuring up potential work or overseeing works that we had undertaken.

The small works usually comprised of small farm access roads, private driveways or minor alterations to factories and mills.

The usual enquiry for these type of works was dealt with initially by Frank who was able to gain an extreme amount of information from just a phone call, it was a joke within the Department that Frank would say Mrs so-and-so needs her drive resurfacing, such a nice woman, been married for 20 years and has had her little finger amputated. All of this information was totally irrelevant but when measuring up the job for estimate we would invariably find that Frank's information was true.

My time attached to this department was mostly spent with Charles measuring potential work and overseeing the work as it progressed and eventually computing the final account. This experience became invaluable when I eventually formed my own small civil engineering contracting company.

The next department that I was attached to was the

estimating department, run by Robert McDade, a wily Scot who had been headhunted by Kenyon as he had the experience of estimating for large contracts within the civil engineering industry. I spent quite a long time working with Mr McDade and was eventually allowed to visit sites that we were tendering for to do the preliminary evaluation. Towards the end of my tenure with Mr McDade we were working on an estimate for the construction of a reinforced concrete dam in the Washburn Valley which would eventually increase water storage for the Yorkshire area. This was probably the biggest undertaking that the company was about to embark on, and I spent a considerable time on the site of the construction of the dam carrying out a tacheometric survey. The estimate was eventually completed and a meeting of the Board of Directors of the Bradford Dyers Association (the company who owned Pavior construction company) and was ultimately responsible for the financing of the same. The results of that meeting was that the decision was made not to proceed submitting the estimate, but McDade was given permission to contact other large contractors who may be interested in McDades estimate and he was able to sell it on. He was bitterly disappointed that all his hard work was not to be used for the benefit of Pavior construction company.

During my time working with both small works and estimating departments, lunchtimes were spent with Mr

McDade, Frank Clare and Jerry Lee and myself playing solo, a game which the three of them taught me and I thoroughly enjoyed my time spent with these much older men.

Chapter 22

McDades **estimating department** was not downhearted for long after the Thruscross reservoir price. But the department was shown to be very successful in obtaining a sub contract on the M6 for the construction of seven culverts and three bridges, the advance works of a nine mile section of the motorway.

The main contract was awarded to Tarmac civil engineering Ltd for the construction of the M6 motorway between junction 16 and junction 20 and a sub contract was awarded to Pavior Construction Company for the advanced works of this section of the motorway. The work was to commence in 1960.

Before staff could be appointed and work commenced an establishment of a site compound and the positioning of the required plant should be carried out, and it was decided that I should be the advance contact to get the ball rolling. I don't think the decision was taken lightly as it was a substantial responsibility for someone so young, however I was dispatched to Sandbach to book a room at the market town tavern in the centre of Sandbach and to receive their daily instructions as to what to expect to arrive and where to locate the various plant and equipment.

A plot of land had been purchased on the B5077 adjacent to where the motorway would cross over. This piece of land would act as the compound where various offices would be erected and plant workshops established. At the same time a team of men were dispatched by head office and instructed to contact me as I would find them accommodation for the period of their work.

Within a couple of days earth moving machinery was sent with police escort and the police were given my details so I could direct them to where the machine was required. With a team of men in the right machines we were now able to strip the site of soil and to establish a hardstanding. As soon as this was achieved sectional buildings were sent to site and the team were engaged in the construction of offices, workshops and canteens etc. The whole area was to be enclosed in an unclimbable fence. The establishment of Civil Engineering sites today would comprise of mobile offices which could be inhabited immediately, fully fitted out and furnished, and would considerably reduce the cost of site establishment. I was quite enjoying the responsibility but obviously being management I was unable to socialise with the workforce, and consequently I felt isolated, so to overcome this isolation I decided that the company could and should allow me to dine well . There was a very well established restaurant called the Old Hall in Sandbach which was only about a mile away from my digs in the Market Tavern. The menu was expensive as was the wine list, but for a couple of weeks I thoroughly enjoyed my evening meals but it was not very long before the financial department at head office realised the amount of money I was spending was not appropriate for my level of pay, and I was told in no uncertain terms to find somewhere cheaper.

The site compound was established in about two weeks and very shortly after that site administration staff including a site clerk was sent to take up residence. About this time I was also informed that I was to remain on site as junior engineer and should find myself some permanent accommodation, I was also told what my accommodation allowance would be. The site clerk Kevin Daley was new to the firm and his employment was for the duration of the works in Cheshire. I had not met Kevin before but as he seemed to know the ropes of being a site clerk so I left the search for suitable accommodation in his capable hands. Within the space of a week he had located a house in Kidsgrove, a suburb of Stoke-on-Trent, which had rooms to let and he suggested that we should take a room each at this establishment. After a week lodging at this address we both decided that it was not suitable and had to look for an alternative, he eventually found one in Crewe which was a terrace house, 90 Queen Street, owned by a widow Lady called Mrs Evans. On the positive side was that the lady was very accommodating, prepared to cook us an evening meal, and the location was reasonably close to the works, on the downside she only had one room to let which had two beds, a bathroom on the half landing, and an outside toilet at the end of the garden. There was no form of heating what so ever in the bedroom, nevertheless Kevin and I decided to take the room. In the event I lived there for 18 months and was quite happy with my first home away from home, and did eventually keep in touch with the lady until her death many years later.

The work was now well underway with the establishment of a site agent and a senior engineer, a general foreman and an ever-increasing labour force as the work got more and more intense.

The agent Geoffrey Palmer was a former Army civil engineer who had extensive knowledge of the type of engineering that we were undertaking. The senior engineer David Johnson was my immediate boss and had the responsibility for setting out, ordering materials and working closely with the general foreman Dan Crossley who in turn had the supervision of the labour force. I worked very closely with David and gained a phenomenal experience from him regarding the type of work that we were engaged in. It was also decided that I should continue my education and I enrolled on the civil engineering course at Stoke Technical College three nights a week and a day release, whilst all this was very hard work and holding down a job as well as the experience gained was invaluable in my future career and in eventually forming my own company.

The work rotor was soon established and David the engineer and I took it in turns to have the weekends off which meant I could travel back to Yorkshire and spend time at home, and when it suited the firm I spent the day in head office reporting on the progress and taking back from the management further instructions as to how the work should proceed on site.

Dan Crossley the general Foreman was a man of great experience and had worked on many large civil engineering sites around the world. He was a big man, had a powerful voice and managed to drive men through fear more than persuasion. On one particular occasion during the construction of the foundations of the bridge over the B5077 his power to motivate the workforce was demonstrated. The bridge foundations had to have very large concrete bases from which the bridge abutments were built. The reason for this was that we were working in the areas where salt was being mined and in the case of major subsidence the jacking facilities of the bridge had to be more than that of normal construction. The large base consisted of two halves with an expansion joint in between the two, one half had to be cast with the formwork on three sides supported against the sides of this excavation, the third side's formwork would have structural steel bracing raked and secured in the base of the excavation to allow the second part of this foundation to be cast against it when a suitable strength had been achieved. This was one of the largest concrete pours I have ever witnessed and it took three concrete plants working for eight hours to produce the amount of concrete required in this enormous base. On the day of the pour the work went well until approximately three quarters of the pour was complete. The end which had the raking shores began to move, and if the movement continued it could be a disaster, and the cost of rectification would be enormous. Dan jumped into the excavation and put his shoulder against the moving formwork, a purely futile gesture but at the same time screamed at the joiners on site to jump down there with him and continue frantically to halt the movement of the formwork. In the event he saved the day as the movement had only been an inch and a half and that could be sawn off when the base had achieved the required strength and the formwork could be removed. Like I said he was a very powerful man.

The work on site carried on more or less to programme. I thoroughly enjoyed my involvement with the work on a major civil engineering project and being away from home we worked all hours, played hard socialising with other staff members and enjoyed my time with my adopted family at 90, Queen Street, Crewe.

I was given increasingly more responsibility and especially during my weekends on while the rest of the management team would be having a weekend off.

We had got to the stage of constructing 16 columns at each side of the Crewe to London railway line which would carry the motorway over the railway. This particular weekend the work seemed to be going well and the joiners working that weekend would be expected to shutter up and cast the kickers, a short section of the column against which the formwork for the full height could be erected. I had set out a line which the joiners had to work from giving them an offset dimension to work to so they could set the kickers in the correct line. I was desperate to get home that weekend and by Saturday lunchtime I had done all the setting out necessary to allow the gang to fix shuttering and cast the kickers. I left the ganger with the responsibility of measuring from the offset line to position the kickers, so I left to spend a weekend at home.

Because it was my weekend on I was allowed to turn in late on Monday morning and by the time I got there I realised that there was something wrong. I was summoned into the agents office who regaled me with everything that I had done wrong during my time working on the M6 which I didn't think was too bad, except that particular weekend the joiners not only had cast the kickers for the 16 columns but had shuttered and cast them to their full height. I should have been there to supervise, in the event they read the offset dimensional wrong and ended up with all 16 in the wrong place and as I arrived they were being demolished.

The outcome of this most severe bollocking was that the agent said he would not employ me ever again and if the decision was left to him he would certainly terminate my employment with the company, which reduced me to tears. However the decision was not left him and he had discussed with the MD that I should return to the office and be found work for the company there.

It was fairly obvious that the measurement made from my offset had been mistakenly made on site and it was my responsibility to make sure that the columns would be cast in the correct position. However I don't think any of the site staff thought the outcome would be that I would be dismissed. So with a heavy heart I said goodbye to all my colleagues on site, after which I went to 90 Queen Street packed my things and said goodbye to Mrs Evans, but I told her I hoped this was not the last time I would stay with her as I hoped to return to work on the M6 again in the near future.

		GBP	
700340	Bread Seeded 800g	1.09	A
700340	Bread Seeded 800g	1.09	A
727483	GREEN THAI / CHAR	2.49	A
9361	FRUIT AND FIBRE	1.29	A
712116	TEABAGS YORKSHIRE	5.49	A
727455	VEG TIKKA / VEG BI	2.29	A
5136	CREAM CRACKERS	0.52	A
7144	Marmalade 454g	0.69	A
43320	Ginger Nuts 300g	0.49	A
723809	TOOTHPASTE	2.49	B
723809	TOOTHPASTE	2.49	B
719736	Bacofoil 10m	2.99	B
725108	CHOC DIGESTIVES	2.65	B
726775	HOBNOBS 255G	1.29	A
73557	COTTAGE/SHEP PIE	2.49	A
86515	Sausage/Liver	2.49	A
71365	Digestives Milk	0.75	B
70948	Oatie Chocolate	0.77	B
71368	Digestives Dark	0.75	B
725823	Lurpak 600g	5.35	A
86514	Hot Pot Lamb/Beef	2.49	A
807346	GRAPES RED	1.79	A
723789	QUICHE/FRITTATA	1.39	A
21965	PIE STEAK/CHICKEN	1.49	A
727656	QUICHE PREMIUM	2.89	A
807593	BANANAS 5PK	0.85	A
807345	GRAPES WHITE	1.79	A
718584	MINI BABY PLUM OTV	1.65	A
809684	PEAR CONFERENCE	1.39	A
807260	APPLE PINK LADY	2.49	A
808378	ORANGES	1.39	A
813778	CHOCEUR 200G	1.99	B
703049	Beer	1.85	B
62309	Wainwright Ale	1.59	B
715492	Ale Theaksto 500ml	1.69	B
66455	ALE 500ML	1.55	B
703048	BEER PROPER JOB	1.69	B
725870	DOMESTOS MIXED	1.49	B
725157	Pizza Takeaway	4.25	A
3319	Whisky 8 Year 70cl	15.99	B
725870	DOMESTOS MIXED	1.49	B
3317	Whisky Hland 70cl	11.75	B
41476	Oil Olive	4.89	A
45613	MILK SEMI 4 PT	1.55	A
722535	HEINZ BEANS 4PK	3.99	A

13:18:18   07/06/23
Card Number: ************4106   00
Debit Mastercard
Merchant ID: **25946
Terminal ID: ****4991
EFT No: 2234

SALE

Your account will be debited
with the total amount shown:

Goods: 115.32
Total: GBP115.32

SOURCE   : CHIP READ

APPROVED
Authorisation Code: 766267

AID: A0000000041010

PIN Verified

Please keep this receipt for your records

CUSTOMER COPY

T o t a l   115.32
45 Items
Card Sales   GBP   115.32

A 00.0% Net   61.35 Vat   0.00
B 20.0% Net   44.98 Vat   8.99
*5587 779/090/003/016 07.06.23 13:18

Thank you for shopping at
Britain's Best Value Supermarket
#AldiEverydayAmazing

Every day, seven young people
aged 13-24 are diagnosed with
cancer. If you can, support
Teenage Cancer Trust by
texting ALDI3 to 70490 to donate £3.

Texts cost the donation amount plus
one standard network rate message.
When you text, Teenage Cancer Trust
may use your telephone number
to reach you by phone or SMS.
If you do not wish to receive
contact, please text ALDINOINFO3

condition for an exchange or refund. Higher value and technical items will have an extended Manufacturer's Warranty. If you experience any problems with this type of product at any time during the Warranty period, please contact the helpline, details of which are on the packaging.

Aldi Stores Limited
Holly Lane
Atherstone
Warwickshire
CV9 2SQ
VAT 813 0534 68

Aldi accepts cash, Maestro, Visa debit and Mastercard debit cards in all stores. American Express®, Visa and Mastercard credit cards accepted in all stores.

MIX
Paper from responsible sources
FSC® C018525

Any item bought in our stores is covered by a no quibble money-back guarantee. If you change your mind, bring it back within 60 days with the receipt and in its original condition for an exchange or refund. Higher value and technical items will have an extended Manufacturer's Warranty. If you experience any problems with this type of product at any time during the Warranty period, please contact the helpline, details of which are on the packaging.

Aldi Stores Limited
Holly Lane
Atherstone
Warwickshire
CV9 2SQ
VAT 813 0534 68

Aldi accepts cash, Maestro, Visa debit and Mastercard debit cards in all stores. American Express®, Visa and Mastercard credit cards accepted in all stores.

MIX
Paper from responsible sources
FSC® C018525

Any item bought in our stores is covered by a no quibble money-back guarantee. If you change your mind, bring it back within 60 days with the receipt and in its original condition for an exchange or refund. Higher value and technical items will have an extended Manufacturer's Warranty. If you experience any problems with this type of product at any time during the Warranty period, please contact the helpline, details of which are on the packaging.

Aldi Stores Limited
Holly Lane
Atherstone
Warwickshire
CV9 2SQ
VAT 813 0534 68

Aldi accepts cash, Maestro, Visa debit and Mastercard debit cards in all stores. American Express®, Visa and Mastercard credit cards accepted in all stores.

MIX
Paper from responsible sources
FSC® C018525

Any item bought in our stores is covered by a no quibble money-back guarantee. If you change your mind, bring it back within 60 days with the receipt and in its original condition for an exchange or refund. Higher value and technical items will have an extended Manufacturer's Warranty. If you experience any problems with this type of product at any time during the Warranty period, please contact the helpline, details of which are on the packaging.

Aldi Stores Limited
Holly Lane
Atherstone
Warwickshire
CV9 2SQ
VAT 813 0534 68

Aldi accepts cash, Maestro, Visa debit and Mastercard debit cards in all stores. American Express®, Visa and Mastercard credit cards accepted in all stores.

MIX
Paper from responsible sources
FSC® C018525

Any item bought in our stores is covered by a no quibble money-back guarantee. If you change your mind, bring it back within 60 days with the receipt and in its original condition for an exchange or refund. Higher value and technical items will have an extended Manufacturer's Warranty. If you experience any problems with this type of product at any time during the Warranty period, please

Chapter 23

It was about lunchtime when I returned to head office in Saltaire and the news of my dismissal from site preceded me and much of the idle chitchat was about what I had done wrong and how I had come to return to the office.

It didn't take me long to get over the shame of having to leave work on the M6 and to start to work for the various other departments as I had done previously. I began to be involved with minor works in and around the area and was able to put my major mistake behind me.

In the typing pool there were three young ladies who were about my age and naturally when the opportunity arose I asked each of them out on a date. Debbie, tall, slim and blonde nicknamed by the men in the yard as' the body' readily accepted my invitation for a drink one evening after work and I quickly realised how she came by her nickname, as a lack of intelligent conversation usually meant that our time was spent in the car parked up in some lay -by. The topic of conversation when I met with the lads usually focused on how far did you get? as with most groups of young men at that time there existed a scale. Ours was from 1 to 5, five being the ultimate sexual experience, but in those days as there was no true safe form of contraception most girls would never go that far.

The other girl, Carol, a dark haired slim and equally attractive girl, who after much persuasion eventually agreed to go out with me on a date. Our time together was much more rewarding as Carol was a good conversationalist and had an opinion on most things, however whenever we did park up the same taboo applied, therefore never achieving the ultimate.

Whenever time permitted between night school and helping out in the pub I usually made a date with either one or the other girls and as Carol had a part-time job as a croupier in a small casino on Fox's corner in Shipley, I was able to kiss Debbie good night and go on to meet Carol after her shift at the casino, and as far as I was concerned this was a very satisfactory arrangement.

Because Pavior construction company was wholly owned by the Bradford Dyers Association and had been restructured to take into account the government's expected expenditure in a motorway network encompassing the whole country, a totally new management team was engaged. The heads of the various departments within this restructuring were headhunted from the biggest and best civil engineering companies in the country. All the foregoing meant that there was considerable rivalry between the new management team and Kenyon, the managing directors idea, in an attempt to defuse this rivalry, was to hold regular get togethers in one of the local pubs after work. They were always good-natured events and a fair amount of alcohol was consumed. These events were not entirely for the management but for anyone working in the office was invited, and on one particular occasion the public house chosen was the Malt Shovel in Baildon. As the gathering was drawing to a close I offered Carol a lift home which she accepted. I decided however to make a slight detour and park up at the side of the road on Baildon Moor, I was hoping for at least a kiss and a cuddle, but Carol had had too much to drink, and when her features took on a pale shade of green she flung open the MG car door and proceeded to be sick, but in so doing managed to grasp hold of the elasticated leather pocket as the door swung open and was able to fill the pocket with the misdirected vomit. Needless to say this cooled both our ardours and left me with a scooping and disinfecting job the next day, nevertheless, the incident was soon forgotten and we continued to see each other for quite some time.

My work in head office took on similar pattern which I experienced when I was last there, I was basically consigned to the engineer Department, but was fortunate enough to experience all the other departments which helped to give me a rounded education.

The intercom made its familiar rapid ringing tone in the engineers drawing office indicating that it was the managing director, I answered and was summoned to his office and the sign on Kenyons door asked me to wait. Unusually I was asked to take a seat, and from that I deduced I was not there for my usual telling off." I will come straight to the point" said Kenyon" the workload on the M6 for the management team is more intense than when you were last there and it seems that the site agent acted a little hastily, so he has made a request that you return to site and take up where you left off as assistant to the site engineer. This change of situation is to take effect immediately and I would appreciate it if you went home and collected what things you need, make contact with your former accommodation, and set off back to Cheshire and be ready for work tomorrow morning on site at the usual 6 a.m. Before you leave indicate to Bradford Institute of Technology that you will be leaving the course and you will be taking up your studies at Stoke Technical College with the usual three nights a week and a day release". I decided to push my luck and ask will this mean an increase in salary, that remark ended the convivial atmosphere and I was left in no certain terms that I was lucky to go back on site after such a monumental cock up last time I was there.

When I arrived back on site I was met by the engineer who was obviously delighted to see me and that his workload was not going to be as intolerable as it had been. From my conversations with the engineer during that first day back I got the impression that apart from the disastrous decision I made with regard to the columns on the motorway, the people in charge were satisfied with the work I had done previously. The work of this section of the M6 was overseen by a firm of independent civil engineers as the workload for the local authority was too great. It was a well-respected worldwide renowned civil engineering specialist and I got on extremely well with the Dutch engineer who was in charge of the section that Pavior Construction Company was responsible for. He was very helpful to me virtually taking me under his wing and explaining the nuances of the work that was being undertaken in intricate detail. During my subsequent work as an engineer I often looked back on what the Dutchman taught me.

Mrs Evans was delighted to see me back and had not let my old room, so I took up where I left off enjoying my time at 90 Queen Street. I spent time in my room on the homework set by the college but still found time to socialise with visits to the local pub with Mrs Evans' new lodger who had taken the room vacated by the site clerk who had now moved on to bigger things.

Even though I was living in Cheshire my thoughts still returned to home and how the pub was doing. I was always interested in art and sculpture, I did in fact take up sculpture in the form of bronze casting for 10 years during my retirement, but I digress so while at Mrs Evans I decided to make a tableau for the Christmas decorations at the pub, and set about forming a wire mesh armature onto which I could form a papier-mâché reindeer. This construction was to be placed above the revolving door at the main entrance to the Brown Cow along with the sleigh and the Santa Claus with presents.

It was good of Mrs Evans to allow me to use the kitchen as making a half size papier-mâché reindeer is a messy process and I was using copious quantities of flour and water as the adhesive to stick newspapers to the wire armature. Once satisfied with the shape I applied sheets of plain white paper onto which I could paint the details of the finished article. The construction of this piece took quite a few weeks but when it was complete and it was my turn to go home on my weekend off, I positioned the reindeer behind the seats of the MG but was unable to close the hood, quite a sight to see a sports car with a reindeer riding in the back.

Christmas was always a busy time for the pub and my grandfather was always keen to decorate the public rooms. This was usually done by a team of window dressers from Lewis's department store, who would take over the pub one morning prior to opening and string festooned decorations from the lights and paint snow scenes on the mirrors and windows, this usually took place a fortnight before Christmas Eve. Although it was some years since I was a member of Whitkirk Church choir I was delighted to see that the choir still sang on the steps in the hall of the Brown Cow with piano accompaniment from Gilliard the choirmaster. One difference to that particular night would be that the choir in cassock and surplice would sing until approximately 11.15 when they would leave the public house to take their positions in church for the Christmas midnight service. This practice usually made church attendance increase considerably as the customers from the public house would follow the choir and make their way into church.

On my weekends at home I took up with the old crowd who met regularly on a Saturday evening in the taproom of the Brown Cow before heading off to some Dance Hall in search of female company. By now the group was beginning to break up as some of the lads were forming permanent relationships which would eventually end up in marriage while others pursued careers further afield so the numbers were dwindling, but I suppose all good things must come to an end.

I still kept in close contact with a few of the old group and five of us decided that we would take a holiday together. Ostend was a chosen destination and a return flight from Yeadon (Leeds/Bradford) airport was booked, this was before passenger flights on jet aircraft were rare and the plane that took us to Ostend was a Dakota, an American built aircraft which was prominently used during World War II to transport soldiers to where the battles were intensifying. Like most people at that time it was our first experience of air travel, except for my one flight to

Jersey with my parents. . Ostend at that time was a popular destination for young people as there were nightclubs and coffee bars which attracted young people from all over Europe. Suffice it to say that a week away from home was very welcome, and all five of us enjoyed the experience.

Other times during my weekends at home usually meant I would be asked to serve at the back of the bar as these times were extremely busy, nevertheless I thoroughly enjoyed it, meeting different people and having time to spend with the regulars who invariably would asked me to have a drink with them, so with free drink and convivial conversation the time passed very quickly.

I usually left very early on the Monday morning to return to my work on the M6.

Chapter 24

On one of my weekends spending time at home away from the site, I was relaxing in the dining kitchen away from the public areas of the Brown Cow, when the intercom phone rang "Get your coat Lad, meet me down in the rear car park, your Grandad's poorly, we're going to have to bring him home". It was about 10 o'clock at night, dark and with a slight drizzle, walking across to the car Dad threw me the keys and said "You drive lad". He had never really taken to driving but realised that in a modern society it was a necessary evil. We both settled down in the front bench seat of the Cresta "Where to?" I said. "Beeston" was the reply as I started the three-litre engine, it was a new vehicle and it was agreed that he and Bertie should have a new car each. Berties was an automatic top of the range Ford Zephyr (he always liked his cars) and Dads was a Vauxhall Cresta beige over sage green. it was now quite evident that Vauxhalls parent company the American General Motors was influencing the design. The Cresta had large fins at the rear, enormous chrome bumper bars front and back and a propensity of chrome everywhere else. It was a column change, a fashion which is now well out of favour.

I drove out of the car park, down Selby road and on towards Leeds getting directions when we neared the Beeston area. Our destination was a brick built middle terrace house, the type that had a half submerged basement room sometimes referred to as a garden room and a flight of four or five stone steps up to the ground floor. The ground floor lights were on and the front door was wide open. Florrie, his wife, had been dead for about four years and Bertie had struck up a relationship with a lady of a similar age, I don't suppose we will ever know whether the relationship was ongoing prior to Florrie's demise, but nevertheless he had gone to see the lady on this particular night, his night off, and there he was sitting upright on a stool at the top of the stone steps silhouetted in the light of the hall. He was his usual dapper, nay sartorial self, wearing a three piece suit, shirt, collar and tie, immaculately polished shoes, overcoat and trilby hat, but it was fairly obvious that he was stone cold dead.

"Have you phoned the Police?" my father said to the lady who was trying to maintain some form of composure, but was clearly upset by both the traumatic experience and her emotional attachment to Bert. "No" she said at which Jack turned on his heels and walked up and down the pavement outside the house. Five minutes later he had obviously made up his mind and returning to confront the lady said "Have you a phone?" "Yes" with a trembling voice," it's here in the front room." So moving past Bertie Jack went to use the phone whilst I sat and waited in the car. About fifteen minutes later he came back, sat down beside me and said "Were waiting lad." "Why, what's the matter" I enquired. "Your Grandads dead and I've just rung the doctor and the undertaker." About half an hour later both Dr Morley, our family doctor who was local to the Brown Cow, and Tom Stevens the local undertaker arrived. Jack immediately got out of the car and was in conversation with the two men. The conversation became more and more heated and the lady more and more distraught looking on from the top of the steps behind Bertie's body. Quite a bizarre scene really I suppose, however it was quite obvious that Jack wanted something that was quite beyond the wit and ability of the two professional men, the undertaker and the GP, nevertheless eventually a deal was struck. Apparently Jack wanted to avoid any apparent scandal that may attach itself to Bertie's impeccable character or at least this was how he had persuaded the GP and the undertaker to go along with this scheme and have the Death Certificate read that Bertie had died at home. The reality I believe was that Jack thought that by doing what he proposed would make certain that the lady in question would have no claim on any part of Bertie's estate. "Come on Lad were taking your Grandad to the undertaker's parlour". We both made our way up the few steps, I taking hold of Bertie's shoulders and Dad his legs and carried him out to the Zephyr which was parked immediately outside the house, and with a little bit of a struggle we were able to slide him into the back seat, sit him up propped against the central arm rest and close the door. Neither Morley nor Tom Stevens would take any part in this but had agreed with my father that should we deliver him to the undertakers establishment in Halton, the next village to Whitkirk. Dr. Morley would issue a Death Certificate which affirmed that Bertie had shook off this mortal coil at his place of residence. Jack felt in Bertie's overcoat pocket, retrieved the car keys and handed them to me" You'll have to drive lad, I can't drive an automatic car." So, as Bertie's Zephyr was automatic I had to drive. In any other circumstances I suppose it would have been quite exciting for an eighteen year old to be able to drive two very expensive motor cars on the same night, one on the way there and one on the way back. My Dad drove off indicating that I should follow. It was now about 1am as he drove across the City of Leeds, I in close pursuit, occasionally glancing in the rear view mirror to see my Grandad propped up still wearing his trilby, being driven by his eldest Grandson at the age of eighteen on his last but one journey. A bizarre experience but nevertheless one that is indelibly printed on my mind, and sure enough the obituary read that Bertie Greaves a prominent Landlord of a large public house had died at home in The Brown Cow.

A week later his coffin was lying in the Gents smoking room, a small room to the left of the main front door of The

Brown Cow. On the other side of Selby Road was Whitkirk Church steadily filling up with mourners who had known Bertie over his 72years of life, a prominent Landlord for most of those years, he had made a lot of acquaintances and was extremely well respected, and amongst them were Directors of Tetleys Brewery and many other Landlords from other parts of the City. Because of the proximity of the church, the six pall bearers carried the coffin out through the front door of the pub, across Selby Road and into the church for the burial service.

I was instructed to stay back and maintain the public house opening, for some silly reason pubs were not allowed to close on their designated hours for any reason whatsoever, so it was I that was standing in the front doorway with no customers except one with a pint of beer in his hand, watching a scene unfold which was quite remarkable. The pallbearers along with the Rev. Cranston Garrett in front of the coffin walking slowly out into the centre of Selby Road which had been closed and traffic diverted down Hollyshaw Lane and into Crossgates. A stream of mourners left the church and were still leaving the church when the coffin arrived at the graveside 250yards further down the road in the graveyard, where four years before my Grandmother Florrie had been interred.

The customer, a regular, but not that regular that he felt it necessary to be part of the cortege, turned to me and said "By hell Bertie, if you could get up now and see this you'd be right proud"

With the death of Bertie as licensee of the Brown Cow, it gave the brewery the opportunity to take back under their control the jewel in Tetleys crown and install a Manager instead of a Tenant which would be more favourable and more profitable for the brewery. All this in spite of the fact that Jack had been virtually responsible for the running of the pub for the last few years of Bertie's life, so it was a bitter disappointment when Jack realised that Tetleys wanted to run the Brown Cow as a managed pub and not offer it as a tenancy. However the Directors of Tetleys did recognise over the last 10 years that my family had been responsible for making this pub a roaring success. They offered Jack an extended period when he was able to continue to run the Brown Cow as a tenant, while offering him the tenancy of other various public houses owned by the brewery as and when they became vacant. So for six months my Mother and Father viewed numerous hostelries and the choice eventually was narrowed down to three. The Duke of Wellington on Wellington Hill on the outskirts of Leeds, the Wheatley at Ben Rhydding near Ilkley and the Red Lion at the crossroads of Whitehall Road between Leeds and Halifax and Bradford Road between Bradford and Huddersfield. Because of it's previously poor performance and reduced rent my father thought that the house had the most potential for change was the Red Lion at Wyke.

A date was agreed when the handover would take place

and two licensed premise valuers would be appointed to carry out the value of fixtures, fittings and stock of both places and to draw up a financial agreement between my Father as the new tenant of the Red Lion at Wyke and Tetleys Brewery. The day chosen was mid winter in 1960 and as I have mentioned previously by now I was living away from home in digs in Crewe and working as a Junior Engineer on the M6 motorway, so to satisfy my employers, and to give as much assistance to my parents with their epic move, it was agreed I should return to the Brown Cow on the evening prior to the move and have a couple of days off from work to help. So on the last day that my father would be licensee landlord of the Brown Cow I was to leave work from the site in Cheshire in the early afternoon and travel home in time for the final farewell from the customers and staff.

In the event the best laid plans did not work out, and by the time I was ready to leave our site compound just outside Crewe at a village called Alsager the weather had taken a turn for the worse with flurries of snow, and my MG TF was not the best equipped vehicle to be travelling in snow across the South Pennines. My usual route, (bearing in mind these were the days long before the M62) took me through Congleton, Chapel en le Frith, Buxton, Glossop and then over Holme Moss (one of the Pennines high passes) into Huddersfield and on to Leeds and eventually home.

By the time I got to Buxton the weather had deteriorated even further, but as Local Authorities were doing their best to keep major roads open I decided to press on, through Chapel and on to Glossop. This is some open hilly terrain but I managed to slip and slide my way eventually arriving in Glossop well above my intended timetable. I was cold, tired and by now fully convinced the canvas roof on the MG did not offer sufficient protection in weather conditions such as these. Still in two minds whether to pack it in and look for somewhere to stay in Glossop, I ventured into the Police station to try to get an update into the state of the roads into Yorkshire (yes these were the days when you could walk into a local Cop Shop). I stood behind a wagon driver also hoping for information on road conditions as he was on his way into Yorkshire. Eavesdropping on the conversation I heard that the only pass open was the Snake Pass from Glossop to Sheffield and that was passable only with extreme care. The driver thanked the Police and told them his decision was to attempt the journey.

"Can I follow you? I said making the decision with my heart and not my head, as I still hoped to be there for my Mum and Dads last night. "What are you driving?" came the question. "An MG TF" I said "You've got to be mad, but I'll keep my eye on you in my mirror." So we set off not wanting any further delay and realising that even the Snake may be closed at any moment. The journey was not without its difficulties, but to give the wagon driver all credit, he managed to negotiate the route under terrible conditions with such professionalism and was even able to keep an eye on my progress close behind. And so it was that the journey which even in the heaviest wagon allowed on British roads would take less than half an hour in good conditions, the wagon driver shook my hand in a lay-by he had just pulled into on the outskirts of Sheffield some 2 hours after leaving Glossop Police station. "Thanks "I said, which didn't really express anything like the gratitude that I felt.

"You're welcome, I think we will be the only two over the pass tonight" was his reply, and with a final wave of gratitude and a thumbs up sign I continued on my journey home.

It was around midnight when I finally banged on the back door of the pub, some ten hours after leaving Alsager. It was Dennis our cellar man who opened the door but it didn't take long for my Mother to throw her arms around me. "Where the hell have you been, we'd given up on you coming tonight."

"Mother it's a long story, how did your last night go?"

"Well, just after we closed, your father fell over a beer crate and has burst a varicose vein in his leg."

So there he was sitting on a stool with his leg propped up and a tourniquet round his thigh, and I said

"This is a bright start to your new future."

Early the next morning the removal van arrived ready to load furniture and all that my mother had packed, which included all the family had accumulated over the last 10 years from the living quarters of the Brown cow to transport it to the Red Lion at Wyke. While all this was going on two teams of licensed premises valuers settled down to the task of agreeing the value of what was to be left behind, one acting for my father and the other acting for Tetleys Brewery, all this included wet stock, fixtures and fittings. The work proceeded well on into the afternoon and in spite of this taking place the new manager had taken up his position and had opened the public house on time.

At about lunchtime my mother and my brother had left along with the removal men to take possession of our new home, and to supervise the location of our furniture and everything else that we had come away with.

Since early that morning two other teams of licensed premises valuers were engaged in agreeing the value of fixtures fittings and wet stock of the Red Lion on behalf of my father and the outgoing tenant, a lady called Billy Naylor who was the previous licensee of the Red Lion.

Back at the Brown Cow my father, Dennis the bar cellar man and I were bringing matters to a close and eventually left mid-afternoon along with our two Alsatian dogs, Flash my dog now knocking on a bit and Caesar my father's favourite, another guard dog.

To say this period of time on that particular day was a traumatic event is an understatement, and it was with a heavy heart and a lot of emotion for the memories of what we were leaving behind as we said goodbye to the Brown Cow and the end of an eventful chapter, nevertheless looking forward to the new adventure.

The Landlord's Son

THE RED LION

Chapter 1

We arrived at the Red Lion to find that my mother and my brother had busied themselves allocating bedrooms and deciding where the furniture for the lounge and the dining kitchen should be located.

With regard to the licensed premises the valuers had agreed a figure, so now all that remained was for Dennis, my Dad and myself to prepare the premises for opening time at 5.30.

The task for the next few months or so was for my Father, Mother and Dennis to make the place a viable business. For myself, back to work on the M6 and for my brother back-to-school.

At about 6 am on the Monday morning I left the Red Lion to return to Cheshire, and of course at that time there was no motorway between Yorkshire and Lancashire, so my route took me through Huddersfield over Holme Moss crossing the Sheffield Manchester Road and onto Glossop. The countryside around here is bleak as it is on the edge of the Peak District National Park and at that time in the morning you don't expect to see anyone, but there on this bleak and unpopulated road was a young woman hitch hiking. I stopped and asked her where she was going and she said she was a nurse at Glossop hospital, had hitch hiked from her home in Sheffield hoping to get to work for the start of her shift at 7am. It transpired she had spent a short period of time with her parents. In today's attitudes to hitch hiking I don't think you would find a young woman alone in that remote area but I eventually dropped her off at Glossop hospital and continued on my journey through Buxton, Congleton, and on to Alsager.

Chapter 2

Life at the Red Lion had now settled into a regular working pattern. The customer base was improving and although little change had been made to the décor my Mum and Dad had great plans for alterations and improvements, but they were prepared to wait to see how things worked out before they invested any more money in the business. The pub was located on a notorious crossroads on the major road between Bradford and Huddersfield and Leeds and Halifax, it was notorious because there was history of a number of serious accidents, and my Dad was interviewed by the local press to find out what his thoughts were on such a dangerous crossroads, his answer was not the best I've heard when promoting a business, he said "Well, we should sell more brandy!"

Being located at the junction of two major highways lunchtime business was brisk with many commercial travellers calling for lunch on their journeys between Yorkshire and Lancashire. The seasons were now changing from autumn to winter and on one particular midweek day a group of regular travellers, and for that matter regular customers, were all in for lunch when the weather turned particularly bad. In a short space of time there was a fair depth of snow outside on the road and it was quite clear that onward travel for these people would not be possible. Amongst these customers was a large man affectionately known as De Kuyper Joe as his regular tipple was De Kuyper Gin. Joe was a milled flour salesman selling to various bakers in Yorkshire and Lancashire. My father and mother at this time had not changed the décor of the main lounge from the previous ownership and one of the feature's of the public house was a large bay window in which a grand piano stood. The customer base on this particular occasion was fairly noisy as it was obvious that the customers were not going to get anything more done today. Amongst all the noise De Kuyper Joe moved across to the piano and began to play, he was the most unlikely classical musician with massive hands, nevertheless within moments he commanded silence as everyone listened to a rendition of Greig's Piano Concerto. The silence continued for a few moments after Joe had finished playing, and then the room erupted with a hearty applause.

The public house was originally established as a coaching inn and to that regard had a large barn and stabling to the rear. This facility was underused as it was only to store bottle crates, and as I explained before my brother at our previous address was interested in the activities of the cattle market, and he decided to continue that interest by rearing a dozen turkeys in the barn. This venture was so successful that by the time they were ready for slaughter for the Christmas table the lightest one was 20lb and the heaviest 30lb. I'm not sure there was a lot of profit in his enterprise, but everyone who purchased one was very satisfied.

I also used part of the barn to restore an old BSA 500 motorcycle which I stripped of most of its extraneous weight and fixed it with a reduction sprocket so I could drive it in the field, a steep plot of land of approximately one acre between the pub car park and the stream known as Pickle Brig which ran under the viaduct and belonged to the Red Lion. Driving this motorbike in the field and falling off it many times cured me of ever wanting a motorcycle on the highway.

At the side of the stream was a public footpath which connected the village of Bailiff Bridge under a viaduct, (now disused) to the railway station at Wyke, and it was this footpath that was a major feature in a story told by Ernest Marshall a weaver from Firth's carpet mill located in Bailiff Bridge. Ernest's nickname was Pablo, a name he was given by the workforce from Firth's carpet mill. On a one day trip to Scarborough, Ernest took up the challenge offered by Pablo's Ice Cream Parlour to anyone who could eat a bucketful of ice cream they could have it for free. After succeeding in devouring the bucket of ice cream, he was, needless to say, very sick on the return journey.

The customers of the Red Lion were an eclectic mix from all walks of life and Ernest could often be seen in conversation with Arthur Smith a multimillionaire who had a nickname Tex derived from his headwear of choice which was a Stetson hat. I recall one of Ernest's stories was when he was courting and took his girl for a walk along Pickle Brig. "Look" said Ernest to his girl, "My mothers given me an orange to eat on our walk" to which the girl who later became his wife said "Oh you only eat oranges when you are pregnant!" Ernest replied "Well put it in your pocket and eat it on the way back".

On the other hand Tex's story I recall was that in his wallet he carried a gold card, he said "I got this card for not paying my bill". Apparently he and his wife Vera had gone on the first world cruise of the QE2 just shortly after her launch. It transpired that after a month away at sea the cruise terminated in Miami and the passengers were booked into the Miami Hilton for a night and then they would catch a flight home to the UK. Tex and his wife were so impressed with the hotel that they decided to stay another couple of days. After the extra two days Tex went to pay his bill, however he was astounded at the amount of money they charged for just two nights and began to create a fuss in the hotel's foyer. The under manager was called to the desk as Tex was creating a disturbance. "What's the trouble?" asked the under manager, Tex replied "I've no trouble as I've got the money, and I'm not prepared to pay this extortionate amount of money" The under manager saw he was getting nowhere and asked Tex if he would step into the manager's office. Still creating a fuss Tex was led into the manager's office and was asked to take a seat to which he said "I can't possibly stay here a moment longer at the rates you charge". "Please sit down" said the manager "And tell me which part of Yorkshire you are from". He had obviously recognised Tex's strong Yorkshire accent. "Leeds", replied Tex. "Well that's a coincidence" said the manager "I was born in North Street in Leeds, so please sit down and we will have a whiskey together". A while later after drinking a substantial amount of the bottle of whiskey and reminiscing about his home town the manager said "Will you stay another couple of days, you will be my guest?" Tex amazed at this said "Why what's the catch?" The manager replied "Tomorrow is carnival day in Miami and I have it in my power to make someone a Freeman of the City, and I would be delighted if I can bestow this honour onto a fellow Yorkshireman".

"So you see" remarked Tex "I got this gold card which says this is to certify that Arthur Smith (Tex) is a Freeman of the city of Miami by not paying my bill!".

Chapter 3

It is now about 18 months since my first appointment in Cheshire and my company's works on the advanced stages of the construction of a short section the motorway were coming to an end. Consequently I was no longer needed on-site and therefore had to return to head office.

I fell into the same routine as when I was last there spending time in the drawing office, drawing bar charts indicating the programme of works for various contracts, preparing estimates and the management of the small contracts. There were also two major contracts under way at the time, one was the construction of the Huddersfield Inner Ring Road and the other was the construction of the first section of the Addingham bypass, neither of which required a full-time setting out engineer and consequently I spent my time between the two. The Huddersfield contract involved the demolition of some buildings to accommodate the line of the new road. This meant that the design of the construction of the carriageway was mainly dependent upon what was found after the demolition and the local authority engineers department would investigate the site and ascertain how the construction of the carriageway should be undertaken. The setting out and management of the works was generally undertaken by the permanent site staff, but occasionally I would be called in to help with setting out the line for the kerb layers to follow. Working in a heavily trafficked urban environment was infinitely different to that of my experience working on the M6 when the line of the motorway was through agricultural land. I was on site on one occasion when there was heavy machinery working in the vicinity, and I and the workforce around me were shocked to hear an almighty explosion. It transpired that one of the machines had struck an existing manhole which housed the electricity supply to the trolleybuses in Huddersfield, and this damage caused all the trolleybuses to come to an abrupt stop. Civil Engineering is never without unexpected incidents.

On the other hand the work on the Addingham bypass was more akin to the work that I was familiar with from working on the M6 as the line of the new road went through agricultural land. The only complicated part of this work was that it required seven culverts within the short length that we were to construct which would be able to take the run-off from Addingham Moor and discharge it into the river Wharfe.

Now permanently based in head office I picked up where I left off with the social life and continued to enjoy the interaction with all the members of staff most of whom were individual characters. The buyer at head office was Arthur Cleary who smoked continuously lighting one cigarette from the stub of the last. He began his day with a raw egg in warm milk and after downing it in one gulp would say to himself "Right Cleary you can now smoke". At Christmas time you couldn't get into Cleary's office for presents given to him by grateful suppliers of materials over the previous 12 months. He being a generous sort would distribute these presents amongst other members of staff.

Apart from civil engineering the company also had a separate surfacing department, it was run totally independent of the civil engineering side apart from the fact that original enquiries and estimates for surfacing was dealt with by the civil engineering staff. The autonomous unit was run by Jack Marcham a well-respected name in surfacing. He was a brusque large man who commanded the respect of the staff under him. His second-in-command was a chap called Jack Gittings, a jovial man always well-dressed in sports jacket, cavalry twill trousers, brogue shoes, check shirt and tie, I always thought he looked as though he was dressed for a day at the races rather than administering the surfacing gangs. The department operated two Barber - Greene paving machines each with a five-man crew. These machines laid tarmacadam usually into layers, base course, and finishing course to specified thicknesses and finishes, at the front of the machine there was a hopper which took the material directly from wagons with heated bodies which brought the material from quarries where the quarried stone and bituminous binder would be mixed. The operation was much quicker than hand laying material with rakes and shovels, but in tricky areas and on narrow footpaths hand laying was still practised. As mentioned before when describing my early introduction to site measuring with John Swales, I referred to surface dressing.

This surfacing department operated two bitumen spray tankers and two 10ton capacity wagons fitted with chipping spreading mechanisms which would regulate the rate of spread of the chippings onto the pre-prepared bitumen sprayed areas during surface dressing operations. This type of work is seasonal, as it depends on warm air temperatures to allow the chippings to be embedded in the pre-sprayed hot bitumen.

Surface dressing is a form of resurfacing carriageways at a much lower cost than actually applying another layer of macadam which gave the existing surface a new lease of life. The measurement of this work left to the engineers department I have already dealt with as it became one aspect of my earlier employment.

There were also two hand laying gangs comprising of five men each along with the necessary tools including a hand controlled motorised roller. Each gang had a van and a trailer which carried the tools. The work that these gangs did was mainly resurfacing of private driveways, but could be available to make up the numbers if the work on machine laid macadam was too much for the existing gangs.

The Department was obviously very profitable but kept itself to itself, consequently I had little to do with them other than to measure up the work at the outset for the Estimating Department and to measure the completed work for the final account.

Working at head office in Shipley meant that I was back living at home with my parents and my brother in the Red Lion, Dennis the bar-cellar man from the Brown Cow took up my father's offer to join us at the Red Lion and to live in and was a valuable member of the team. Also living with us was Flash my Alsatian, now an old dog and in recent years with me working away from home I did not spend as much time with him as I had when he was younger, but I did take him a walk whenever I found the time. Eventually the time came when it was cruel to keep him alive and on one Monday morning as I left for work I looked in the car rear mirror and saw him stood there with my Dad and with tears streaming down my face I knew this would be the last time I would see my best friend.

Chapter 4

A**lthough we still** had Caesar the Alsatian, a couple of weeks later my mum bought a chocolate miniature poodle as there had always been a dog in her life and this was no time to do without one. Chico as she called him was certainly not a replacement for Flash, but as in the last few years of his life my mum looked after him while I was away and consequently now she felt the need for a canine companion.

Even though we had moved away from Whitkirk I still kept in contact with Charlie and we both decided we would retrace our journey to Scotland, however, Charlie invited a friend of his who I was also acquainted with, Gerald Thompson who lived in Halton a district between Whitkirk and Crossgates both suburbs of Leeds. So in 1962, the three of us attended a party at the nurses home attached to the Leeds general infirmary. The party ended quite late, but it seemed a good idea to set off in my car for a weeks holiday. Our first stop in the early hours of the morning was in Glasgow where we availed ourselves of a hearty breakfast in a transport cafe. The trip was very pleasant, but not memorable. However, some time after our return, Gerald wanted to show the video he had taken on holiday. On the night chosen Charlie was busy, consequently, Gerald and Janice his then girlfriend came to the Red Lion to show off his film. It was just the three of us in our upstairs lounge and we spent a pleasant evening having a couple of drinks and discussing what took place on holiday. Janice came across as a very likeable girl with a good sense of humour and was very attractive. I thought at the time how fortunate Gerald was to have such a girlfriend, but thought nothing more about it as they seemed to be in a strong relationship and when that evening came to a close I didn't expect to see either of them again. I had no idea at the time that two years later Janice and I would meet.

Mum and Dad continued with the work making the Red Lion more to their liking, it meant the Grand piano had to go, new decorations, new curtains and furnishings. All the changes were carried out over a fairly long period of time and it became evident to the regular customers that my mother and father were prepared to spend money making the place more comfortable. Around this time the pub was frequented at lunchtimes by the carpet salesman and their clients from Firths carpet mill in Bailiff Bridge 2 miles away. It was becoming increasingly obvious as the work progressed that the redecoration and furnishings were going to be of a very high standard, consequently one of the salesmen from Firths mill approached my parents and asked if they were intending to carpet the lounge area, as he could see an opportunity to use the pub as a place where they could bring potential clients and be able to show them the type of product Firth's made. As the change in décor continued, Firths were prepared to offer to make a high-quality carpet known as a double manson, in a style that suited my mother's taste and they would be prepared to offer it at a much reduced price from what they would normally sell it. It was an offer that my parents couldn't pass up and in the ensuing years proved valuable to Firths as a show piece.

Although the pub was in a rural location it was still close to manufacturers producing carpets, apart from Firths. Two miles in the other direction was a mill which produced Lambtex Rugs and the managing director Norman Burnett was a regular customer. Norman particularly enjoyed the early evening group of customers who found the Red Lion a place to wind down after a hard days work.

A domino school was quickly formed and while not a lot of money changed hands the game was always competitive. The game took place in a small area of the lounge adjacent to the bar, but should the games continue beyond an hour after opening the players were relegated to the tap room (By now reader, you must be familiar with the fact that public houses offered facilities for two types of clientele. Those dressed up and out for an evening and those not so well dressed just there for a drink after work) as the lounge clientele began to arrive.

Around this time pubs were a place to socialise, their popularity reached an all-time high as television had not developed and did not offer the extensive range of entertainment it now holds.

Bearing in mind the foregoing I vividly recall an occasion when my parents had taken a holiday and I was left in charge of running the pub while they were away. To cover for them I took time off work. One particular evening the domino school was well underway when it became time for those inappropriately dressed to leave the lounge area and either go home or resettle in the taproom. One particular regular decided in spite of inappropriate dress he was not prepared to move and an argument ensued in which this customer maintained that my Father would not ask him to move to the taproom. I moved from behind the bar and tried to reason with the man but he became violent and swung a punch. Fortunately I ducked and he missed and I reciprocated flooring the man, two of his companions then joined in and the situation looked as though it was about to get ugly, but fortunately two regular customers came to my aid and eventually the situation resolved with the man leaving threatening never to return.

I was sure nevertheless that my father would have been glad of the decision I made as I was able to maintain an atmosphere where people come out for an evening of social discourse in pleasant surroundings and to be able to purchase an alcoholic drink of their choice. This is what all landlords hope to achieve at a time when public houses were the main source of evening entertainment.

Chapter 5

I **had decided that** now was probably the time to concentrate more on my education than travelling around the country on various civil engineering projects that Pavior Construction were undertaking. Consequently I actively looked for a new position with another employer meaning I was able to work close to my home and also to the technical college in Bradford which about this time changed its name to a College of Advanced Technology. The Department of Civil Engineering was developing a good reputation and with that in mind I enrolled for a course which they offered as three nights a week and one day which would require release from my employer.

After sending my CV to Civil Engineering contractors who were operating in the area. I was eventually interviewed and offered the post of assistant engineer with Wimpey who were constructing multistorey flats in an area of Bradford off Manchester Road.

It was with a heavy heart that I tendered my resignation from the company which had given me start in my chosen profession, and I quickly took up the post offered by Wimpey.

It was obvious from the outset that the company

structure was entirely different to that of my former employer. Wimpey was a national company engaged in projects all over the UK and also some abroad. The structure of the company meant that its administration would be easier if their operation was split into different departments. The one with its headquarters in Leeds was Department 13 which was responsible for administering the site on which I was to work.

The site accommodation was very similar to that established during the construction of the M6 having sectional offices built on site to accommodate a Site Agent, Engineers, and secure buildings for storage of small materials and tools, the whole of which was enclosed behind an unclimbable fence. There was also one particular office comprised of a wooden hut but furnished better than the rest, which was the office of the clerk of works appointed by Bradford City Council to oversee that Wimpey's adhered to the original estimate and building regulations.

The site management team included an agent/site manager responsible for the overall running of the site. The Site Clerk was responsible for keeping records of all employees whose salary depended on time keeping. All these details including time sheets for individual employees and other information regarding the works progress from which an interim account could be prepared for payment from the local authority was given to the Leeds Office.

For a site as large as the one we were working on financial calculations would be administered by the Leeds office.

There was an overall site Foreman who was in charge of the various gangs and also had specific responsibility for the quality of the work.

There was a ground works ganger, he looked after the excavation of the foundations underground drainage and the construction of carriageways and the landscaping of the area after the buildings were complete.

Other trades each had a foreman or a charge hand. These included bricklaying, concreting, carpentry, and joinery. All other works on site was done by subcontractors mechanical and electrical engineering plumbing and painting and decorating.

My responsibility was setting out of all works including roadworks drainage. I was also given the task of the overall responsibility for quality control.

I quickly became acquainted with the ways that Wimpey liked to run things and enjoyed my time on this urban building site. I soon settled into my routine of working four days and the Saturday morning and further education continued three nights a week and a whole day at Bradford's Institute of Technology Civil Engineering department. My course was going quite well and I enjoyed the lectures, but invariably my homework was returned with an inordinate amount of red ink with the comment that the content was correct the spelling was appalling, my undiagnosed dyslexia being responsible for the red ink. (I Thank God now for the dictation programme on my computer). The course was frequented by a good mix of young men pursuing an engineering career that was divided into those that worked for local authorities and those who worked for contractors. For many years after the course had finished and I continued to work in the industry I came across many of the friends had made at Bradford Institute of Technology.

I was in the clerk of works office just before one particular exam which I was apprehensive about, and during the conversation about my further education he said that he was an amateur hypnotist and with hypnotism, he could relax my apprehension. It was a couple of days later that I actually agreed to be hypnotised nevertheless, I was very sceptical but went along with him and was eventually put under. The hypnotic session to my mind was really short, but it seemed to work because I went into the exam with confidence and passed. However, I still had reservations about its effectiveness and thought no more about it. Many years later when I was no longer employed by Wimpey and my company was working on some surfacing for a Wimpey building site, I was approached by a foreman and eventually recognised him as Barry McDonagh one of the foreman on the site in Manchester Road, Bradford, many years before. We reminisced about the time we worked together and he reminded me of the clerk of works hypnotic abilities. I had no idea that it was common knowledge on site that the clerk of works was an amateur hypnotist and was able to perform and produce a hypnotic state. Barry McDonagh, mentioned the subject of me being put under hypnosis to relax me for a particular stressful exam. I was quite surprised that he knew all about the session and he just smiled and said that word had got round the whole site and there was an awful lot of the labour force looking in through the window of the clerk of works office during the hypnotic session. I suppose after all those years I had to accept that I was hypnotised and my scepticism was unfounded. Barry told me it was an hour's entertainment and that an awful lot of the labour force had enjoyed it, further destroying my original thoughts that the session was really short and in actual fact had lasted an hour.

Chapter 6

Occasionally we make decisions that eventually prove to be entirely wrong and I am no exception to that rule. Alec Issigonis had designed a revolutionary new small motorcar, it was known as the Morris Mini Minor, it had a transverse engine and front wheel drive, it was very basic inside but it was extremely efficient and cheap to run. The decision I made was to sell the MG and purchase a Mini, the car became very popular and even some of the younger royals had purchased one so it seemed a good idea at the time. With hindsight I should have kept my MG as in today's market it is worth an inordinate amount of money, but what is done is done. I was now living with my parents in the Red lion and commuting to work on the Manchester Road site of Wimpey's. It was now approaching winter 1962 and on one Monday morning it snowed sufficiently to cause traffic chaos, but the Mini with its front wheel drive performed extremely well in snowy conditions, and I was pleased with my new car and its ability to cope with these conditions. About a mile away from the site where I was working the driver of a car behind lost control and slid straight into the back of my car. I got out to assess the damage and to exchange insurance details between myself and the other driver after which I began to kick the other car in order to separate them as I was wearing heavy site boots. We managed to push the other car to the side of the road, but because of the transverse engine and front wheel drive, I was able to continue on my journey to work. Later that evening I was working behind the bar when a customer came up and said" I saw you lose your temper in the middle of Manchester Road and kick the hell out of another car". I smiled and explained that it was necessary in order to separate the two vehicles after the collision. I'm not sure he believed me.

By now, the pub was doing reasonably well and my Dad felt confident enough to take my Mother on holiday. They had already made some good friends who frequented the Red Lion on a regular basis. There was a group from Halifax who were about the same age as my Mum and Dad and ran small businesses. A collective decision was made to go as a group on a Mediterranean cruise. So it was that Harry and Mary Holroyd, a small shopkeeper from Halifax, John and Mary Drake a haulage contractor and coal merchant also from Halifax, and Bobby Briggs and Joan a large transport cafe owner from Drighlington, along with my mother and father had a fortnight's holiday cruising the Mediterranean. I was pleased that they felt confident that they could leave the running of the public house to Dennis and I. During this particular period of my working behind the bar, a customer came in looking to have a conversation with me and it turned out that he was a civil engineering contractor who was looking to develop his business. He explained that he had a company employing approximately 50 men engaged mainly in laying ducts for the GPO, they also carried out a small amount of building works mainly property redevelopment and they also had a plant hire business, all administered from one base located in Wibsey, a suburb of Bradford. The company was split into two halves run by two directors both Ernest Moulson's sons, one responsible for the civil engineering side and one for the plant hire side. He had heard of me and followed my career so far and said he would like to offer me a job expanding the building and civil engineering side. I was to be answerable only to Billy Moulson, but I would have the freedom to expand the company in any direction I chose. He hinted at a salary and should my involvement turn out to be successful, I would be offered a directorship.

I was flattered by the offer, but had to explain that I was currently employed by Wimpey and had a day a week release to continue with my studies at the Bradford Institute of Technology, nevertheless, I assured him that I would give it serious consideration.

Living at home and not in digs working on the M6 my social life improved immeasurably, I still saw one or two of my old pals from the Brown Cow, at the same time pursuing interests in the fairer sex. Closer to home in those days young people got together in dance halls and the Mecca was where I met Sandra, a tall, slim extremely good dancer who put up with my mediocre performance on the dance floor. Over the next couple of years we saw each other once a week on average, and spent our time either in the Mecca or in public houses, but invariably parked up in some field gate and doing what 18 to 20 year olds do. On one particular occasion I recall we were parked in a gate entrance just off the main carriageway and in the time we were there had not noticed that it had begun to snow. When it became time to go home, the car wouldn't move no matter how hard Sandra pushed. We sat in the car with the heater on for some considerable time wondering what our next move should be. It was well past midnight when a police car came along and stopped, noticing our predicament the two policemen got out of their patrol car and pushed my car out of the snow and onto the highway. Neither of them spoke, they just got back in their patrol car and drove off. I doubt if that course of action would have been taken by the police of today.

Certain momentous events have some significance and bearing on your own life, and on one such occasion I was out with Sandra in a public house when the landlord came up with the news that John F. Kennedy had been assassinated. This small detail gives credence to the cliché 'where were you when Kennedy was assassinated', and I can remember it to this day.

As monogamy was not part of my vocabulary at round this time I also struck up a relationship with a girl from the village above where the Red Lion was located. Penny was petite, attractive, didn't dance, but enjoyed our social activities going to public houses or the to the pictures. I also occasionally saw the girls who worked at Pavior construction company and struck up a mutually convenient social relationship with a typist from Wimpey's Leeds office. Being footloose and fancy free suited me very well.

As I was now nearing my 21st birthday, my mother decided that we should celebrate the fact with a big party and threw herself into the task of arranging such a celebration, and finding suitable venues which would accommodate the number of people that my mother thought we should invite. The Prospect Hall in Cleckheaton, a small town close to where the Red lion was located, was the chosen venue, a DJ was fixed up and a buffet menu decided upon.

Mother produced a guest list which included an awful lot of my friends and one or two of my parents close friends.

The party was a great success. I suppose at my age larger gatherings were not top of the list at the time, but the event marked my coming-of-age. One negative result at the event was that the DJ at the end of the evening suggested I should dance with a girl of my choice and I chose Sandra because of her dancing ability. With hindsight, a foolish decision, as it upset my relationship with Penny. I should have asked my mother.

Being the licensee of a public house meant that opportunities to socialise were limited but on the odd occasion my mother and father went out for an evening. It invariably meant, to my mothers disappointment, that they would visit other licensed premises. This gave them the opportunity to see how the opposition was doing and what ideas other licencees had to attract custom. There was also a Licensed Victuallers Association and my grandfather, when he was alive, was a staunch member becoming President, however, my father never did join but still enjoyed meeting other licensees. The Red Lion being located close to Bradford meant that invariably on their nights off, they would visit public houses in the Bradford area. One such public house, located in the West Bowling suburb of Bradford, was run by Ken Jubb an ex-rugby league player whose son Alan, also a well-known rugby league player was the licensee of a public house in the centre of Bradford called The Crown. Ken and Alan along with their wives made social visits to the Red Lion and became family friends. Because of this relationship, I once asked Alan if I could borrow his membership card of a nightclub in Bradford called the Lyceum to which he willingly agreed, this gave me the opportunity to take Sandra out somewhere different. The Lyceum was a club that offered a cabaret show with dining and gambling in the form of roulette and blackjack. I had no knowledge of the fact that the Lyceum was allegedly operating outside the law, but on the night I chose to take Sandra the club was raided. A Police inspector walked onto the stage and informed everyone present that the club was about to close, that each exit had a policeman who would be taking names and addresses of those who were present in the club. This action taken by the police made me very nervous as they had not made clear what they intended to do with the information gathered, especially when I was there on someone else's membership card who was a well known licensee in the local area, and any decisions taken by the police could impact on the renewal of his licence. Fully expecting to have to spend the night in the cells, Sandra and I got up to leave and were stopped at the door and asked to produce the membership card. I handed the officer Alan Jubb's membership card to which he looked directly at me and said "Alan your appearance has changed drastically" and after a short period of silence whispered "On your way lad, when I next see Alan I will tell him his name did not appear on the list of attendees to the Lyceum that evening". With a sigh of relief, Sandra and I got into my car and I drove home, just another experience to add to my list.

Still living at home with my parents in the Red Lion I spent a lot of my spare time working behind the bar and because I had developed a liking for beer I was often asked by a customer I was serving if I would like a drink and on the occasions I accepted it was always a half pint. In those days. My capacity for drinking was much larger than it is today and on occasions I would drink a yard of ale (a glass a yard long with a bulb at one end and an open collar at the other which held 2.4 pints) the trick was to drink it all in one go without putting the glass down which I managed on many occasions!.

Some of my time while working behind the bar of the Red Lion were spent in the taproom. This room attracted a good clientele on their way home from work who just wanted a pint before going home. I got on well with the customers and struck up a friendship with a man about my age called Jack. At around the same time Charlie got in touch to say it's time we had another holiday, I readily agreed and we decided on the south coast. Jack also expressed an interest and asked if he could join us so we got together and decided on a date, but did not pre-book anywhere and took pot luck at places to stay. We drove down South in one day and arrived in Torbay and proceeded to book into the Torbay hotel, much to Charlie's disappointment as he said he had a limited amount of cash available. Consequently, it was agreed that we would have a night of luxury and look for a hostel in our next place to stay.

The accommodation in the Torbay hotel was excellent and again much to Charlie's horror we decided to dine there as well. We had taken a reasonable change of clothes and consequently enjoyed the evening dining in salubrious surroundings. The next morning after a hearty breakfast, we set off further around the coast to Weymouth, where we found an excellent bed-and-breakfast and spent the evening exploring Weymouth and its pubs. After a 'Full English' we decided our next stop should be Bournemouth, a town which had a large youth hostel so we booked in, showered, changed and set out for the evening to find somewhere to eat and for some entertainment afterwards. Sampling the delights of Bournemouth took on longer than we anticipated so when we returned to the hostel with a few drinks inside us we found that we had been locked out. Charlie's solution to this was to sing at the top of his voice enjoying giving everyone a rendition of a popular song, lights were lit and after much grumbling we were let in.

As there is no food provided in such establishments it is left to the residents to purchase their own ingredients and take advantage of the kitchen and its equipment. After Jack nipped out to the nearest corner shop he returned with sufficient food for a hearty breakfast, however, after last night's rendition of the popular song sung at Charlie's most high-volume meant that we were greeted by the rest of the hostlers with some hostility. Consequently, we finished breakfast quickly and moved on to our next place. A short distance round the coast was Southhampton and our early arrival gave us ample opportunity to explore the the port. We hired a motor boat and were able to see the departure of two of the world's largest liners, The United States of America and the Queen Mary, fortunately our motor boat was well away from these two massive ships, nevertheless we still had to negotiate the wash created by them, then on to Portsmouth and the naval dockyard. In port at that time were a lot of her Majesty's fleet and amongst them an aircraft carrier. After such an eventful day we decided to stay in Portsmouth and quickly found a bed-and-breakfast. We then headed off to London the next morning which was to be the conclusion of our trip. We found another youth hostel which we stayed in for two nights taking in most of the regular places of interest before returning back to God's own county, a pleasant trip was had by all.

Chapter 7

Working on the multi-storey flat development in Bradford continued, which I mostly enjoyed but certain aspects of health and safety in those days were ignored and one of the tasks of setting out was to make sure that the wall plate to which the roof timbers would be fixed was level. I decided that the best way to carry this work out was to find a junction of four walls on which I could set up the instrument and have a chain man hold the staff on the various points which we needed to set the level. My chain man on most occasions was a young Pakistani boy called Raj, who was frightened of heights, but to his credit he managed to climb around the roof sections holding the staff where he was instructed, but his trembling made the reading of the figures on the staff quite difficult.

Further transgressions of health and safety were carried out by the pouring gang, men responsible for mixing and filling the shutters with a material particularly specified by Wimpey's design of no fines concrete, the main constituents of which were cement and gravel with little or no sand. This left the resulting wall looking like a well-known chocolate and nut bar. The construction did offer improved insulation and when the external walls were rendered with a waterproof material giving a pleasing finish and the internal walls were plastered, the whole system proved to be a quick and easy form of construction of high-rise blocks of flats.

The pouring gang apart from ignoring health and safety regulations when working at high-level, regularly threw a spanner (an actual spanner) in the works of the machines mixing the concrete, which meant that a fitter had to be called out from head office to repair it, usually resulting in the work having to be carried out late, therefore meaning an increase in salary of the pouring gang. My involvement with this particular labour force was never very good as my responsibility was quality control of the material they produced and to improve accuracy. I used to put different coloured pieces of sticking plaster on the weigh scales dial indicating when various items should be added to the mix. All this was brought to a head when the concrete produced on-site was subject to testing by the production of a test cube of concrete mixed on that day. A steel mould of 150 mm x 150 mm x 150 mm in which a sample of the concrete mix could be made, well compacted by a steel rod which would produce a dense concrete cube, this would be crushed in a laboratory registering the strength required to crush it. These tests are carried out at 7 days and then at 28 days when the concrete is expected to reach its maximum compressive strength. One of these test cubes, representing a first floor of a five-storey block when crushed had failed to achieve the working strength, and as a result remedial work had to take place. The consequential result in the enquiry suggested that I was at fault being responsible for quality control even though this particular batch of concrete was mixed by the pouring gang working in overtime when I was not on site, attending my evening course at Bradford College of advanced technology.

As the company preferred to side with labourers earning four times my salary, because of the overtime they were able to work and were exonerated from any responsibility I decided that it was time for me to part company with Wimpey's.

Fortunately, around this time Ernest Moulson who ran a small building and civil engineering company and who was a regular customer of the Red Lion, had suggested on more than one occasion that I should join his company and that if I did there would be a potential for directorship if the increase in turnover of the company was down to my own efforts.

My letter of resignation was submitted to the management of Department 13 of Wimpey Construction and immediately the overall construction manager "Mick Loosely" let it be known that he was disappointed I was to leave and urged me to reconsider. I said the decision was not his and the chief engineer of this branch of Wimpey's company had the responsibility of accepting my resignation or negotiating terms which I could accept to continue my employment with them. In the event, Mr Thorpe the chief engineer took three weeks to venture out to site to discuss the prospect of my continued employment, this action only reinforced my determination to leave.

Before I took up employment with my new company, Charlie got in touch to say that he and two others who had enjoyed our holiday abroad in Ostend were considering another continental holiday, and that they had favoured a package for a two-week break at a coastal town in Yugoslavia named Opatija. After looking at the brochure Charlie sent me and agreeing with my new employer that my start date would be two weeks later than was originally intended, I readily agreed to join him, Chris Mabbott my cousin, and John Abram's. The package included flight from Manchester on a Lockheed Super Constellation aircraft which was easily recognisable as there were three rudders on the tail and four propeller driven engines mounted on the wings. This aircraft was the forerunner of jet propelled aircraft. The package also included all transfers and three star hotel accommodation. The transfer inclusion was important as the Iron Curtain still existed and the nearest airport to our destination was Trieste in Italy, and featured a coach journey across the Iron Curtain into Yugoslavia and onto our destination, a distance of 105 km. After leaving the airport the coach quickly arrived at the checkpoint where a passport inspection took place on board. However, much to the rest of the passengers consternation, John Abrams had in the last year let his hair grow to shoulder length and his passport photograph did not bear any resemblance to him. The armed guard escorted John out of the coach and had him standing against the checkpoint building with his arms above his head. An hour later the armed guard decided that the facial resemblance was sufficient to allow him to pass and a great sigh of relief was heard throughout the coach. Opatija turned out to be an ideal place for a summer vacation, and we four lads took advantage of the sun, sand, and sea. We also took advantage of the extremely favourable currency rate. We often played cards in an evening which always created a stir amongst the locals, as the pot of money was full of five Dinar notes valued to us as approximately one shilling each. We also hired a motor boat and met lots of girls of a similar age from all over Europe. The holiday was a success, however halfway through the holiday we persuaded John to have his hair cut very short, such an important undertaking attracted quite a few locals to look through the barbers window at the spectacle, as men with long hair was unheard of at the time and not seen in Yugoslavia. On our return journey we suffered the same treatment at the checkpoint because of Johns altered appearance, he was once again removed from the coach by an armed guard which resulted in a half hour delay. The journey home was horrendous as the Super Constellation was limited to a certain height and had to fly through some severe turbulence resulting in Chris throwing up. However we were all delighted to arrive back in the UK.

I started with Ernest W Moulson and Sons Ltd. the following week at a much improved salary and with direct control of the way we should expand the company.

Chapter 8

The **Red Lion** was now fully furnished and had built up a reputation as a venue for customers who required some where with elegant surroundings, comfortable enough to go to dressed up and to meet up with friends to enjoy a night out with drinks. Public houses wanting to attract clients today would need to offer good food, an extensive menu and good wines as people's social activities had changed, but at the time my parents ran the Red Lion food was not offered except on some Sundays when a seafood barrow would be set up in the entrance hall with a range of fish and shellfish which customers could purchase either to take home or would be served along with a salad to be consumed on the premises. This practice is developed into what is now known as gastro pubs where quality meals are served at lunch and dinner time.

On one occasion my father was approached by a policeman from the Bradford constabulary who was looking for a venue that would serve a buffet meal at a time after the public house was closed. The reason for the police enquiry was that the Bradford constabulary, along with many other police forces had benefited from the fundraising efforts of a popular entertainment group at the time known as the George Mitchell Black-and-White Minstrel Show, coupled with the television Toppers a girls dance troupe. Their fundraising efforts contributed a substantial sum to police force benefit charities over the years.

The reason for this policeman's enquiry was that whilst the black-and-white minstrels and the dance troupe were appearing at the Bradford Alhambra, the police force wanted to throw an after show party as a thank you to the Minstrels for all the work they had put into raising money for their benevolent fund. My father's agreement to this special evening would mean him applying for an extended licence for a particular day . The commitment would mean staff working overtime, some in the preparation of a suitable buffet and others required for serving the drinks. This party would be attended by all the members of the show and some of the off-duty policemen who would be able to enjoy a relaxed evening. Eventually a date was agreed and my father would charge the police for the buffet and drinks consumed.

The party would start at 11 pm and there was a considerable number of guests expected.

As I was living at home at the time, then obviously I would be expected to help on the night. My recollection of the event was that it was a great success as the performers arrived just after the show in Bradford had closed, some still in costume, and a number of off duty policemen. An electronic keyboard was set up and the Television Toppers did their routine . Further entertainment was provided by John Boulter, a famous tenor, who sang songs from their repertoire. John Boulter was still in make-up claiming that he actually couldn't get it off but other members of the cast had changed out of costume . However, the highlight of the evening's entertainment was Neville King, a ventriloquist act who had been appearing at the Alhambra with the black-and-white minstrels. At the time Neville's famous act was a little old man as his ventriloquist's dummy, who was slightly risque and eventually had to be put back in his box where Neville was able to make it sound as though the old man was still speaking inside the box pleading to be let out.

But on this particular occasion Neville had brought one of his other dummies. Covering his right arm was a large penis, and at his elbow were a pair of testicles and Neville was able to make this penis talk about its experiences amongst the glitterati at the time, to say it brought the house down was an understatement. The party ended at around 3 AM and both the entertainers and the police were delighted with what my mother had provided as buffet and the way the extra staff had looked after the party goers.

Chapter 9

Ernest **W Molson** and Sons Ltd is located in Wibsey a suburb of Bradford . Ernest himself lived in a detached house on the main road through the village about 40 yards away from his yard and offices. The yard itself was situated in approximately half an acre and the offices were previously a row of stone built terrace houses. The directors of the company, along with Ernest, were his two sons, Billy Moulson looked after the building and civil engineering side, and John Moulson who operated a plant hire business. The civil side's main activity was the laying of GPO ducting, which carried telecommunications cables. The building side operated two gangs each consisting of a foreman tradesman, one other tradesman and two labourers. The work tended to be small contracts for the local authority and sub contract work for the larger contractors. The business had been established many years before when Ernest was a young man and this development was entirely down to him.

Ernest was a larger-than-life character, a big man recognised by his country style clothing and a large trilby hat, he was well-known in the village of Wibsey but also in much of Bradford as he had been a councillor and at the time of my employment was an alderman of the city.

One other peculiarity about Ernest was that he wore a large diamond ring and when asked why he wore such a ostentatious piece of jewellery he said "Its an insurance that I would be able to pay the men if things got tight".

I had very little to do with the plant hire side of the firm, my responsibility was to the construction side directly answerable to Billy Moulson. I was given an office in one of the terrace houses that formed the head office with all the basic facilities I needed to estimate for new contracts, engaging a workforce, and carrying out the contracts which we were awarded. I quickly fitted into the organisation and thoroughly enjoyed the company structure. I was mainly left to my own devices and realised that I would be judged on my efforts to increase the turnover of the building side of the business.

Within the first three months I had managed to secure a couple of reasonably sized building contracts for the local authority and got the company included on the list of contractors for the CEGB who were about to embark on a programme for the construction of primary electricity distribution substations. Because of the increasing demand for electricity, transmission of electric power with high voltages would be more efficient than the infrastructure that existed at the time.

The work needed for these primary substations required civil engineering and building skills which my new company was perfectly suited for.

It wasn't very long before we landed a contract to construct a primary substation on an industrial site in Brighouse, and we were able to put one of Moulson's general foremen in charge whose gang were skilled to carry out the work required.

Jack Swarovski soon proved that we had the right man for the job and in the initial stages the CEGB were pleased with both the quality and the progress, however, the ordering and supply of materials required was in the hands of the existing head office staff and was woefully inadequate. This led to the work falling well behind the required schedule.

This problem eventually came to a head, when according to the submitted programme the works were weeks behind schedule, which meant the resident engineer referred the problem to the regional management of the CEGB and that eventually was transferred to the CEGB head offices in Guildford. Adherence to the programme for the construction of these primary substations was of paramount importance as it was linked directly to developments of main power stations, which would mean that the high voltages could be transmitted to the new primary substations. This technique improved the efficiency of electricity distribution throughout the country. To see the problem for himself, one of the directors of the CEGB flew to Yorkshire and I arranged to pick him up to transfer him to the site offices. I knew we were in trouble and in anticipation I asked if one of the directors i.e. one of Earnest Molson's sons could attend the meeting. At the allotted time for the start of the meeting it seemed that I was going to have to answer the concerns on my own. I had no defence and at the back of my mind could only offer assurances that the situation would improve and that we would endeavour to catch up on lost time. The response to my offer seemed not to allay any of their fears and that it was becoming increasingly evident that the possibility of being asked to tender for future work was becoming remote.

Halfway through this meeting there was a knock on the site office door and in walked Ernest with this 10 gallon hat and his leather working boots covered in pig muck. This type of attire was standard for Ernest because one of his many interests was his pig farm. " Don't mind me", said Ernest after I had introduced him as the chairman and managing director of my company. The meeting comprised of the National Director, the Regional Director, the resident engineer, and the clerk of works, who were attending the meeting on behalf of the CEGB.

Ernest took a seat next to me and I was beginning to despair of my company's prospects of future work when all of a sudden the conversation turned round to discussing a problem Ernest had with a poorly boar pig. To this day I shall never know how Ernest managed to turn such a disastrous meeting around and allay the fears of the CEGB. Eventually the meeting broke up and Ernest suggested I should entertain the CEGB representatives to an expensive lunch. The Shibden Mill Inn, a public house with a reputation for excellent food in convivial surroundings was chosen, and I was well acquainted with the owner manager who was able to accommodate us at short notice.

The delay was improved upon and the work was completed on time to an acceptable high standard and we were regularly invited to tender for future work.

That day I learned a lot from Ernest in how to defuse a situation which could have had a disastrous effect on our future relationship with the CEGB.

Towards the end of the Brighouse contract I was working late on a final account to be submitted to the CEGB. It was a pleasant summers evening and I was very surprised to see Ernest drive up to ostensibly see how I was getting on. We sat on the curb at the edge of the carriageway into the site, drinking a cup of coffee from my flask which I had taken as I knew I would be some time. It was then that Ernest revealed that he had just left a meeting at Birkby's brickworks in Low Moor, a suburb of Bradford, and he wanted to tell someone he had just bought the brickworks lock stock and barrel. I was flattered that he had chosen me to be the first to know that his little business empire was growing, but then he was like that.

Chapter 10

The **Red Lion** by now was established the way my parents wanted it, and the changes paid off as the pub was becoming busier and busier, and whilst not in the same league as the Brown Cow, was making my parents a good living. Public houses in semirural locations depended on customers who were prepared to drive short distances for a night out, and because of the elegant comfortable furnishings and the quality of the well-kept beer It began to attract people from the small towns within a radius of approximately 10 miles. As mentioned before one group of people, businessmen with their wives from Halifax, made it their regular, and amongst this group was a coal merchant, John Drake, and on one evening he mentioned to me while I was working behind the bar that there was a cottage for sale in Northowram, a suburb of Halifax, and this property was ripe for development. In spite of enjoying my employment with the companies I've already mentioned, I always had at the back of my mind that I would like to form my own building and civil engineering company and the conversion of this cottage may be the first rung on the ladder.

Northowram is a village located on top of a hill

exposed to the elements, but it had all the necessary facilities such as three public houses, a small parade of shops which included a post office and newsagents and the greengrocer. There was also a butchers shop housed in its own building and the Co-operative store towards the far end of the village accommodated in its own premises. There was a church and a chapel and housed in a large disused quarry a structural steel manufacturer. Most of the buildings were built of hard sandstone representative of this area, also this semi-detached cottage that was for sale built of the same materials.

The cottage had one room on the ground floor, a flight of stairs leading to a single room on the first floor, and a tiny area under the stairs housing a sink with one cold tap. Small gardens to the front and rear and at the bottom of the front garden there was an external toilet. The property was approached by a short unmade road, which passed a group of six terraced houses on the right, a detached farmhouse on the left, and led to a large field at the rear. I was later to find out that the accommodation which existed in this cottage was home to a mother, father and seven children, however did they manage?.

The property was on offer for sale at the price of £400 and bearing in mind at the time, cottages offering much more comfortable accommodation would be sold for around £2000. The structure itself was sound and built of coursed punched face stone and a stone slate roof. It had one entrance door to the front and two stone mullioned windows to give the only light to both floors. The rear of the cottage had no openings. Internally the only form of heating was one small open fireplace on which coal would be burnt. Gas was connected to the property which provided the only form of artificial light. This in my opinion formed an excellent opportunity for development with a small kitchen extension to the rear, two bedrooms and a small bathroom on the first floor and the rerouting of the staircase to give access to the proposed kitchen extension.

I approached David Parkin, a joiner, who was a member of the Brown Cow group of friends, if he would be interested in carrying out the work and have a share of the profits when it was sold. This seemed to be a good idea. Consequently I purchased the building, however shortly after the work started David Parkin was offered a job in Canada which he decided to take leaving me with the responsibility of finding out how I should complete the work.

I drew up plans for the single-storey kitchen extension, the change of drainage to accommodate the proposed kitchen and bathroom and obtained planning permission.

Chapter 11

A **round this time,** my social life with my current girlfriends had taken a downturn. The original group of lads that met in the taproom of the Brown Cow broke up because of commitments to work and an improvement in their careers. Had they continued I would have been an infrequent socialiser with my working away from the area, and even now living with my parents in the Red Lion it was too far to return to Whitkirk for a night out, nevertheless my friendship with Charlie remained and we saw each other on odd occasions. One such occasion we met in Leeds, I had just finished with a current girl and Charlie was able to meet me as his regular girlfriend Marjorie, a nurse, was working nights. We met in one of the centre of town pubs and then decided that we would finish the evening at the new Mecca dance hall. We were in the bar when the announcement that the last dance was about to take place. We wandered from the bar, which was above the dance floor and on reaching the bottom of the staircase immediately decided that we would break up a couple of girls dancing together. The girl I asked to dance said "Hello Rodney how's life treating you?" and the ensuing conversation meant that she knew of me but I had no idea who she was. Not wanting to be found out, I continued the conversation as though we had knowledge of each other, asking certain pertinent questions, such as 'are you living in the same place'?. Do you still work for such and such, but eventually I had to admit that I didn't know who she was. Her name was Janice Scott and it appeared that she lived in Halton a suburb of Leeds close to Whitkirk and she knew me as she attended the church at which I was formerly a Chorister and was located opposite the Brown Cow. She had seen me around in my MG sports car usually with my Alsatian as a passenger before my parents moved to the Red Lion. She also reminded me that two years ago she came to the Red Lion with her then boyfriend Gerald Thomson to show the photographs taken when we had holidayed together in Scotland.

When the dance finished I offered to give her a lift home to which she readily agreed, and as we said good night to each other I gave her both my works and home phone numbers to arrange another date.

My work with Ernest W Moulson was becoming busier as we were landing further contracts to construct primary substations for the CEGB. One particular substation was located in Holmfield a suburb of Halifax, and the land on which it was to be constructed required foundations located on piles driven into the ground on which large concrete bases would be constructed to support the 200 ton Transformers. The setting out of this work meant that

I was to be very involved with the job at its early stages.

To my surprise during this time Janice had contacted me on my home phone to see if I would like to meet up with her and I readily agreed and she was able to give me her works telephone number as the family did not have a telephone at home. I was very attracted to her, but thought my contacting her was pointless as I believed she was already in a relationship with Gerald, but it transpired that Janice had broken up with Gerald months earlier. A place and time was agreed and I was quite flattered that she had wanted to see me again. Unfortunately, the day before we were to meet I had to cancel as my parents had arranged a night out and I was needed to work in the pub. Being bitterly disappointed I thought that any future relationship had been put in jeopardy. The pub was particularly busy on the night my mother and father had the night off and to my surprise, in the midst of a busy evening Janice appeared in the lounge bar. To say I was pleased was an understatement, I got her a drink and a place to sit and promised to take her home when the pub closed. She had made quite a commitment as it was a journey of about 20 miles and required a change of buses in the centre of Leeds.

From that moment on we experienced a state of mind which I'm pleased to say comes to lots of human beings, we fell in love, and as I sit writing this 56 years later, we still are.

Over the next few months our courtship went in the right direction, we met regularly and it became increasingly obvious that we wished to spend our life together and I eventually popped the question and Janice's immediate response was yes.

There was, however, a slight hitch in our ongoing relationship as Janice was already committed to a trip to Canada with her best friend Wendy to spend time with Wendy's relations in various locations in that vast country. Our relationship by now was so strong that Janice said if I didn't want her to go, she would cancel the arrangements, and of course I agreed that she should go on this momentous holiday, but in truth I was very disappointed that I would not see my fiance for a month. When love takes over rational thought goes out of the window and my imagination ran wild assuming all sorts of scenarios that could occur when we were apart from each other for a month, and I assumed there would be romantic locations on this holiday of a lifetime presenting an opportunity for Janice to meet someone else and break off our engagement.

In the short period of time from my proposal to the date on which Janice would leave for her trip to Canada we saw each other fairly regularly, at least two or three times a week, and in that period of time I had told Janice of my mother's generous offer to use one of my grandmothers diamond rings as the basis for an engagement ring.

One of the regular customers of the Red Lion was John

Kennedy, an international diamond merchant who worked for a manufacturing jeweller in Sheffield. On numerous occasions on his return from trips to Antwerp, he would call in the pub for a drink and would show me gemstones he had purchased. These stones were kept in a small leather purse attached by a chain to a belt loop on his trousers. I could never understand why he would use this method of security for such small but expensive gemstones but it would mean that there would be easy access when it came to demonstrating his purchases to Customs. Janice and I met him privately and discussed our requirements for an engagement ring using my grandmothers diamond ring and manufacturing a diamond cluster with a moderately large diamond at the centre. Not knowing much about such trinkets, I was advised by John that this was a most popular style and he was sure that Janice would be delighted with the outcome. The ring would be made while she was away and I would present it to her on her return.

Because of my living at home I was often required to help at the back of the bar, this along with my work and the improvement of the cottage meant that my commitment to my further education was not what it should be. It was quite clear that the educational route chosen by me, without much more dedication to what I was currently giving, would not lead to my becoming a chartered engineer, so for that reason I decided that my work experience and the practical knowledge gained so far meant I was well qualified to fulfil what I was employed for at Ernest W Moulson Ltd.

There were two main gangs, each with a general foreman within the Moulson labour force, one I have all ready mentioned was involved with the construction of the CEGB primary substation in Brighouse, the other headed up by a general foreman called Harold Reynolds, a man steeped in construction and with many years of experience. It didn't take long for me to appreciate Harold's ability.

The company had landed a contract for the construction of a fire station in Odsal, Bradford.

It was evident that Harold and his gang of men would be ideally suited to carry out the work.

Under Harold's leadership the work progressed extremely well and to the satisfaction of the engineer and clerk of works from Bradford City Council. The design of this particular building had one gable wall to be built in York stone and Harold was the man to build it. It was obvious from the start of my relationship with Harold that he was a man I could admire, he kept his tools in perfect condition and expected his men to demonstrate the same commitment to the work. Just to further his authority he maintained a separate office on site in which he always took his lunchtime breaks away from the rest of the labour force, he was fastidious with hygiene, thoroughly washing his hands and eating the lunch his wife had prepared earlier for him, always with a knife and fork and a napkin. This kind of commitment was unusual in an industry where men were carrying out dirty jobs.

As the work on the construction progressed, the York stone gable was reaching full height when one day while I was on site a bottle green Rolls-Royce stopped at the site entrance and the chauffeur was dispatched to have a word with me. He asked who was constructing the York stone wall and would he be prepared to have a word with his principal who was sitting in the back of the Rolls-Royce. I mentioned this to Harold and he walked across to have a word with this passenger, and was invited to sit in the back of the of the car to continue the conversation. 15 minutes later, Harold walked back across the site to have a word with me. He said, "You'll never guess who that was". "No I won't" I said," but I'm sure you're about to tell me". It transpired that the Rolls-Royce belonged to John Laing, the CEO of one of the largest construction companies in the UK.

"He has just offered me a job, saying he was very impressed with the work on the wall of the gable of the fire station. His company has just been awarded the reconstruction of part of the Bank of England in London and he would like me to go as foreman and oversee the construction of the stonework. The job required that this work be of such a high standard, and he had not failed to notice the quality of the work on this site.

"What did you say?" thinking that I was about to lose

one of the best foreman I've ever come across, Harold said that he was happy where he was now, and no matter how much money John Laing was offering he was staying right here.

That was typical of this gentleman of the construction industry.

In spite of our age difference Harold and I became friends, and with our wives saw each other socially.

Because of my relationship with Harold, it seemed natural for me to ask him if he would be prepared at the weekends to carry out the building works on my cottage, to which he readily agreed. I was to project manage the scheme locating other tradesmen and the materials to carry out the work. The result was a property offering reasonable accommodation and should easily achieve the price we originally estimated at the outset of these works.

Chapter 12

Just before **Janice** was about to leave on her epic holiday to Canada she asked me again if she should consider cancelling the trip as our relationship and our commitment to each other was serious, a difficult decision had to be made, but I reiterated that this was a trip of a lifetime and she should take the opportunity and that the month she would be away would soon pass. So on 1 May 1966 Janice left for her holiday in Canada with her close friend Wendy. Never having experienced before what being in love with someone meant I was not prepared for how badly our separation would affect me. The first few days of being without her made me so miserable that I could not concentrate on anything I was doing. It became fairly obvious to people around me that I was beside myself desperate to receive a letter from her, this of course long before mobile phones put people in touch with each other no matter where they were in the world. After the first five days of separation my mother realising I was desperate for news, rang me at work to tell me that a letter had arrived, and I couldn't wait to get home that evening to read it. From its content I realised that Janice was missing me as much as I was missing her. I did what I am not accustomed to doing and wrote back to her immediately. I have mentioned before whilst I was never diagnosed as being dyslexic, but having since read up about the condition I realise because I am an atrocious speller and I have difficulty identifying right from left, I am convinced that I am dyslexic. In my further education and employment, I was able to hide my dyslexia most of the time. Nevertheless, I overcame my embarrassment and wrote a lengthy tome which Janice's return letter pointed out the amount of spelling mistakes I had made, but she was delighted to receive the communication. There were four letters from each of us throughout the month she was away, with each demonstrating how much we wanted to be with each other. The rest of the month dragged on slowly and I couldn't wait for her return.

It was on 30 May 1966, Janice 's 22nd birthday I was waiting with Janice's mother and father, Mary and George on Leeds City station platform for the arrival of her train from London. As soon as she disembarked from the carriage I ran the length of the platform to throw my arms around her and she did the same, and before her mother caught us up I showed Janice the ring, but she said that "the job has to be done right, so you must speak to my father and ask for his approval ".

George Scott, a very amenable, well liked man by all who came into contact with him was an ambulance driver serving Leeds General Infirmary. I was no stranger to

George as over the last few months we spent time in the company of both parents. The outcome of my meeting with George to ask for his daughter's hand in marriage went moderately well, and I went down on one knee and formally asked Janice to marry me and slipped the engagement ring on her finger. Both George and Mary had come to realise that Janice would make her own mind up when it came to such a momentous decision.

Now the engagement was official and we were involved in discussions as to where and when the wedding should take place. It was fairly obvious that we also needed to make a decision where we were to live together. I had already shown Janice the cottage in Northowram which was now virtually complete with fitted kitchen and bathroom, and all that was required now was furniture. I did tentatively make a suggestion that it would make financial sense if we lived there as our starter home together. Janice was not entirely against the proposal, but we decided that we should involve both our parents to seek their approval. My mother was all in favour of the idea as it would be near enough for her to visit, however Mary's first remarks were "Why do you want to live in Halifax, it's all Co-ops and Chapels?" Another disappointment to Janice's mother would be that it was quite some distance away from where she lived. Janice and I both realised the problem, and consequently started looking for alternatives. It seemed that we both favoured a cottage and it would have to be near enough for me to commute to Wibsey, and for Janice to get to her work place in Leeds. After looking at many estate agents advertised properties we found one that would suit our requirements, which was up for sale by auction. The location was Leathley, a sought-after rural area which offered easy access to Leeds, Bradford and Harrogate. Having made all the required preparations we attended the auction with a maximum figure that we could afford, however we were astounded when eventually the property was sold for three times the amount we had in mind. It became increasingly obvious that my property in Northworam would be mortgage free, cheap to run and also be an ideal starter property. Eventually, both parents agreed, and that as a wedding present my parents would buy us an Ercol dining table and chairs and Janice's parents would buy a matching Welsh dresser, as this was the furniture we both liked and it suited the cottage ideally. We bought a carpet square for the lounge covering the sections of exposed floor with imitation parquet tiles, and on the now rerouted wooden staircase we used a carpet sample collection with a different colour on each tread. In the period between engagement and marriage I made a fitted wardrobe for the front bedroom and we were able to purchase a double bed, which only just fitted in against the wall nearest the window. We became fully aware of how small the room was when on our first winter we realised that because the windows were single glazed, we were able to scratch the frost off the inside of the glass without getting out of bed. Getting dressed followed the same routine taking it in turns to stand in the small space between the bed and the dividing wall between the two bedrooms. These delights only became evident after we were married and living together in our cottage.

As our time in preparing the cottage for our moving in was coming to a close it seemed a good idea to take a weeks holiday together, along with a couple of friends Stuart and Barbara, who were of a similar age and they also were about to make the ultimate commitment in marriage. Now Janice was spending more and more time at the Red Lion, our mutual acquaintances tended to come from that area. We decided on the south coast for our break as Stewart had a wealthy uncle who was developing expensive and exclusive houses close to the sea in Bognor Regis. Stuart's uncle Bill had a large house actually on the beach and accommodation was available. We left early on Saturday morning in my car with the intention of driving to Bognor Regis expecting to arrive around dinner time and to stay with uncle Bill and his new wife for a couple of days and then moving on to Bournemouth. Uncle Bill's place was just as impressive as Stuart had described, his house was a large bungalow which had steps down onto the beach. His development just behind his house was a gated complex with large expensive properties built of materials widely used in the area, and the site had its own licensed club.

After introductions we were offered a drink and then shown two large bedrooms, one for Stuart and I and the other for Barbara and Janice, and we all agreed that proprieties should be adhered to, in fact, we maintained this principle the whole holiday. We spent three days with Bill and his wife Carol enjoying glorious sunshine diving in the sea, taking advantage of the beach frontage and thoroughly enjoying his hospitality . Carol enjoyed Barbara and Janice's company and she was able to show the girls around Bognor Regis.

We thanked Bill very much for his hospitality and moved on to the Chine hotel in Boscombe near Bournemouth, a place where I had stayed with my parents years before. The accommodation was excellent and we availed ourselves of dinner, bed and breakfast which didn't disappoint and a good time was had by all.

Chapter 13

My **employment with** Ernest W Moulson was eventually paying off and because the CEGB was still embarking on improving the distribution of electricity around the country, we managed to land another contract for the building of a primary substation in Harrogate. This was much the same layout with the same reinforced concrete structures, looking like rugby goalposts which would receive the incoming overhead cables. Large concrete bases to support the 200 ton transformers around which would be built brick blast walls. There would also be a switchgear administration building and the whole site would be surrounded by unclimbable fencing . The ground around the structures would be surfaced in loose gravel because footfall in these areas was not very regular, and access to the structures once commissioned would be heavily monitored by an electrical engineer standing by. Moulson had already built two substations to a similar pattern.

The fact that the size and weight of the electrical equipment was huge meant that we had to reinforce existing drainage culverts on the access road into the site so that the 200 ton transformers would not crush them.

The Landlord's Son

It was many years later when I flew on a 747 jumbo jet that the in-flight information stated that fully laden, the aircraft would weigh 400 ton, the weight of two of the transformers, to this day I am amazed how such an aircraft can fly.

Because the company was based in Wibsey the labour force had to be transported from Moulson's yard to the Harrogate site, however health and safety regulations which existed at the time allowed the practice of carrying workmen with a wooden shed which could be lifted onto the back of the wagon. Rules in force today would not allow this practice to be carried out. On one particular morning I arrived early on site and was waiting for the arrival of the workforce when it became obvious that something had occurred to delay them. I decided to drive the route that they would have taken to work, and when I arrived on the Leeds Harrogate road just before Pannal, I noticed that there was a police presence directing traffic around an incident. On closer inspection there were two police cars with blue flashing lights and our wagon in the midst of all this mayhem with a car embedded in the front of it with only the rear half visible. This was obviously a major incident and I pulled up behind a police car and made myself known as the site manager expecting the workforce to arrive an hour earlier. The police informed me that the driver of the private car had been pronounced dead at the scene, fortunately all the men and wagon driver had not sustained any injuries, nevertheless this accident had really upset them all. One of the officers then relayed to me that the pathologist on-site had ascertained that the driver of the private car had died at the wheel at the top of the hill and because the vehicle was totally out of control it had rammed into the wagon at full speed.

Ernest W Moulson Ltd turnover per annum had increased substantially during my period of employment, and I felt the time was right to remind Ernest that he had promised me a directorship should my involvement with the business prove to be successful. Ernest said he would convene a board meeting to discuss the matter and would be in touch fairly soon. A few days later I was asked to visit Ernest in his home and at the outset it was fairly obvious that a directorship would not be in the offing. My reply, as I'm sure Ernest expected, was that I would hand in my notice, and in the ensuing months, would seek alternative employment. I felt both he and I were disappointed but my ambition within the industry was greater than what was on offer.

Chapter 14

I immediately sent my CV to local companies who would possibly benefit from my being employed by them. One of the companies I contacted was Cawood Wharton, a large company involved in the haulage of quarried stone and coal but they also had a civil engineering side which was involved in the construction of primary substations for the CEGB, an area of civil engineering that I was fairly familiar with. Prior to me attending an interview, they had obviously contacted the regional management of the CEGB to see what my capabilities were. The outcome of all the foregoing was that I was offered a position of site engineer responsible to the chief engineer Mr Grumberg.

On 15 July 1966 I started with Cawood Wharton as soon as my notice with Ernest W Molson Ltd. had expired. It was obvious that my new company had a much larger association with the CEGB, which included sites in the north-east and in Lancashire. I quickly fell into my role and enjoyed every aspect of it except one, that my letters had to be handwritten and given to a copy typist for typing on the company's letterhead. As I have already intimated my handwriting was illegible and my spelling appalling, but I soon found a way around this. As the company's current policy was that if I was writing communications from site I was allowed to dictate my letters over the phone. But if I worked in the office, the typists would only accept a handwritten copy. I managed to get around this problem, when working in head office that I would walk down to the local telephone box and phone in my dictation.

I was mainly involved with two sites for the CEGB, one in Seaham, County Durham and the other in Lytham, St Annes, Lancashire. I made two visits a week to each site being involved with setting out, ordering of materials and liaising how the construction had progressed since my last visit with the general foreman on both sites.

Although the Cawood Wharton company head office was in Harrogate, I was able to work from home for the majority of my time as I would visit sites directly rather than attend the head office. All this meant I spent more time at home as I did not need to commute to Harrogate prior to starting work.

My courtship with Janice continued with her being able to occasionally stay overnight at the Red Lion when Dennis our live- in bar cellar man's bedroom was free when he took time off to visit his relatives in Leeds.

A private staircase accessed only from a rear door or a door behind the bar led to the first floor accommodation. At the top of this staircase to the left was my bedroom, and further down the corridor was my parents room . At a junction to the left was a small office and Dennis's bedroom and to the right was a large lounge. The rest of the accommodation was on the right-hand side being a kitchen /dining room. Some times when the rest of the household was asleep I was able to sneak in to the room that Janice was occupying for a sneaky cuddle, and on one occasion I heard my mother's poodle, Chico, who slept in their room, barking, followed by my mother's voice saying "Shush Chico, it's only Rodney." It was fairly obvious to her that I would take advantage of the situation and visit Janice for a good night kiss.

Chapter 15

N**ow settled and** happy in my new employment and
with a date set for our wedding my future was looking
extremely bright. But around the corner was a change, a
phone call from my mother told me that my father had had
a heart-attack and was in Dewsbury Hospital's intensive
care ward. I immediately applied for leave of absence on
compassionate grounds with my new employer, which was
gladly granted, I assured them that my absence would be
no longer than a week as I realised that my father would
not come out of hospital to run the Red Lion again. All
that remained was to give notice to Tetleys Brewery that
my father because of ill-health would like to break the
tenancy, and I would have to go through the procedure
of closing down the public house, and find my parents
somewhere to live.

On arriving home, I found my mother in bits, I asked
Dennis to look after the pub and I took my mother to
the hospital to see how my father was doing. Reasonably
assured by the staff at the hospital that my father would
recover but would be unable to return to work, we started to
put the wheels in motion to relinquish the tenancy and set
a date for our departure. After contacting Tetleys brewery

they were very sympathetic to our plight and said that we could have relief manager at short notice, consequently, a date was set for us to leave. The next item on the agenda was to find somewhere to live, and having perused what was available locally, my mother selected two houses that we should inspect. The first one was on the Halifax Road, Odsal, Bradford, a large stone semi detached property built in the 30s, well maintained, but for some reason or other neither my mother nor I thought it would be their new home. The second one was a property in Birkenshaw, which had all the facilities within walking distance, a butcher's shop, post office, chemists, greengrocers and a co-operative grocery store. The house was a reasonably modern detached property built in the 60s in a line of five houses with a public footpath to open fields less than 30 yards away, good for dog walks. The row of houses was set at right angles to the main road which offered some privacy from the traffic, the accommodation was a lounge, reasonable sized kitchen, dining room, and a ground floor loo, the first floor accommodation was three bedrooms and a boxroom and a bathroom. There was an integral garage, and a small garden, and it was ideal for my Mum and Dad when he came out of hospital. It was offered with vacant possession, which suited this situation. We made an offer which was accepted, and a furniture removal company was engaged and all this happened within the space of a few days.

The day I was dreading soon arrived, word got around amongst past and present customers, friends, relations and those involved with the licensed trade including one of Tetleys directors, all of which meant that our last evening would be extremely busy. Janice came to help behind the bar and the moment arrived when I had to call time and with tears streaming down my face I rang the bell and called time for the last time with thoughts of my father not being present on this momentous occasion. The end of two generations involvement in the licensed trade, with Janice and Mum giving me a hug. Suddenly the whole place erupted with the singing of Auld Lang Syne.

The party atmosphere continued and everybody in the pub wanted to express their good wishes for the future and the return to good health for my father. I moved across the bar to have a word with the director of Tetleys, who had known both my father and grandfather over the years and I asked him if he would like a memento of the occasion, he said he would like the ice bucket that we had in use, which was a round red globe with a white inner lining. Between the inner and outer shell was a filling of polystyrene beads to keep the ice from melting and the lid was of the same construction. I asked Janice if she would empty the ice and dry the bucket so we could give the man his present. Such occasions as this last night never pass without some humorous incident, and Janice eager to please dropped the ice bucket which hit the floor and burst into 100 pieces.

"Never mind" said the director" I shall go away with very fond memories of you, your father and grandfather, It is certainly an end of an era".

Epilogue

N**ow the landlord** is no longer a landlord, my story is almost come to an an end, but the morning after the last night the valuation had to take place between valuers representing my father and valuers representing Tetleys Brewery. As I have already said licensed premise valuers are sometimes appointed to represent the brewery. Other times they are appointed to represent the tenant, which means, in my opinion that the balance is weighted in favour of the brewery. This being the case that I am handling for my father in hospital is no exception, whilst the wet stock valuation is what it is, fixtures and fittings are left to the discretion of the valuers. I sat in on the discussions mainly as an observer, but when it came to the public lounge carpet I was furious that the price agreed was a fraction of its value. This carpet was manufactured for the Red Lion by Firths Carpets whose mill was less than 2 miles away as a one off special so that Firths would be able to bring potential customers to see how such a quality carpet would stand up to heavy traffic. It was clear that my protestations were being ignored and I felt that I was letting my parents down to allow the value of this item to be virtually written off. I refused to accept the value and was so incensed that I stood up and left the meeting, leaving them in no uncertain terms that I was disappointed. This action seemed to have done the trick, as one of the valuers came out to find me extremely distressed in the public house car park to inform me that after reconsidering the situation a value was agreed, close to its real value.

The rest of the day my mother, my brother and I dealt with the business of moving furniture and belongings to my parents new-home. We eventually were ready to leave with just a few items and the two dogs loaded in my father's car, and with a friend of mine who drove my car. We left but not before we had said our goodbyes to Dennis with grateful thanks for all he had done for my parents and my grandparents over the years. He left with sadness which he expressed in a tearful goodbye and hugs all round. I hoped his redundancy package that my mother and father had agreed would go some way to help him finding a new role in life .

After such a momentous week I returned to work for Cawood Wharton and life returned to normal.

Within the space of one year I had formed my own Civil Engineering company and ran it successfully until my retirement in 2006.

Two weeks later, my father came out of hospital to his new home and in a short time was back to a reasonable standard of health and was able to do short walks with the dogs.

Janice and her mother made preparations for our

wedding, a date was set, the church booked and the venue for the reception chosen.

In the short time I had worked for Cawood Wharton I had obviously impressed the management as I was promoted from Site Engineer to Area Supervisor with an increase in salary on 29 May 1967, three days before Janice and I were married.

THE END

Acknowledgements

To my wife Janice for all the time she has spent correcting my spelling and grammar. And to my son Antony in helping me produce the front and back cover.